DARING DELIVERERS

Lessons on Leadership from the Book of Judges

BY
OLLIE E. GIBBS, ED.D.

Purposeful Design Publications is the publishing division of the Association of Christian Schools International (ACSI) and is committed to the ministry of Christian school education, to enable Christian educators and schools worldwide to effectively prepare students for life. As the publisher of textbooks, trade books, and other educational resources within ACSI, Purposeful Design Publications strives to produce biblically sound materials that reflect Christian scholarship and stewardship and that address the identified needs of Christian schools around the world.

Printed in the United States of America
15 14 13 12 11 10 09 08 07 06   5 6 7

Gibbs, Ollie E.
    Daring deliverers: Lessons from the time of the judges
    ISBN 1-58331-117-3   Student edition   Catalog #7056

Cover Design: Matt Garmany

Purposeful Design Publications
A Division of ACSI
PO Box 65130 • Colorado Springs, CO 80962-5130
Customer Service: 800/367-0798 • Website: www.acsi.org

DEDICATION

To Tomorrow's Christian Leaders

TABLE OF CONTENTS

DARING DELIVERERS

GOD IS IN CONTROL OF HISTORY

God is in control of history. He who created the world has not let the world move out from under His supreme guidance at any time. This does not mean all that happens is pleasing to God. Much is merely permitted, but still—God is in charge. This is not only true for Biblical history, but for secular history as well. Since the world began, nothing has taken God by surprise.

It is for this reason that you are about to embark upon an exciting journey. Although your journey will take you back in time over three thousand years, the lessons you will learn are as current as today's news.

There are many unique periods in the history of the world. One of these is the four-hundred-year "period of the judges." During this time, Israel confronted six of the most powerful and influential nations on earth and emerged victorious. However, Israel was not victorious in its own strength. God raised up judges—deliverers— who led Israel to victory.

It is the story of these *Daring Deliverers* that is the focus of this course. While their stories are indeed important, the lessons we can learn from their successes and failures are even more significant.

It is time to begin our journey. May God challenge and instruct you as we take this journey together.

Ollie E. Gibbs, Ed.D.

CHAPTER ONE

Why Are They Called Daring Deliverers?

God Is in Control of History

Have you ever wondered why God included certain books as part of the Bible? For centuries, Bible scholars have debated whether or not certain books of the Bible should have been included. If you were given a list of all sixty-six books of the Bible, would you be able to explain why God included each of these books?

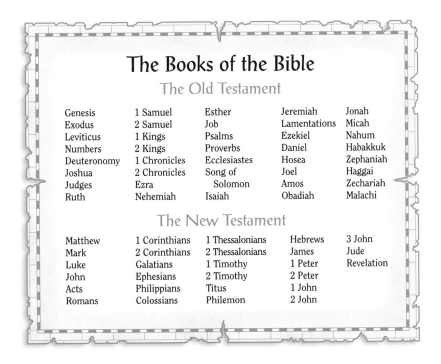

The Books of the Bible

The Old Testament

Genesis	1 Samuel	Esther	Jeremiah	Jonah
Exodus	2 Samuel	Job	Lamentations	Micah
Leviticus	1 Kings	Psalms	Ezekiel	Nahum
Numbers	2 Kings	Proverbs	Daniel	Habakkuk
Deuteronomy	1 Chronicles	Ecclesiastes	Hosea	Zephaniah
Joshua	2 Chronicles	Song of	Joel	Haggai
Judges	Ezra	Solomon	Amos	Zechariah
Ruth	Nehemiah	Isaiah	Obadiah	Malachi

The New Testament

Matthew	1 Corinthians	1 Thessalonians	Hebrews	3 John
Mark	2 Corinthians	2 Thessalonians	James	Jude
Luke	Galatians	1 Timothy	1 Peter	Revelation
John	Ephesians	2 Timothy	2 Peter	
Acts	Philippians	Titus	1 John	
Romans	Colossians	Philemon	2 John	

Even though we may not always understand why, God has a reason for everything He does. The same God who created this universe, including you, has never allowed the world to move out from under

His guidance. Sometimes it may seem like things are out of control around us, but remember that God is always in control. He is never taken by surprise.

It should not surprise you that God does have a reason for every book in the Bible. Before we begin our study of the *Daring Deliverers* described in the book of Judges, it is important to know why God included this particular book as part of the Bible. As you will quickly see, the book of Judges is a clear reminder that God is in total control of history.

What Was the "Period of the Judges"?

The book of Judges is the seventh book of the Old Testament. It is an important bridge between two very important times in the history of the nation of Israel. The first important period, described in Genesis through Joshua, explains the beginning of the nation of Israel, how the nation became so large, and then how the Israelites reached the Promised Land.

The second important period in Israel's history was called the "kingdom period." Described in the books of 1 and 2 Samuel, 1 and 2 Kings, and 1 and 2 Chronicles, it was a time when the nation was directly under the rule of kings—some good and some evil. The "period of the judges" refers to the time between Israel's arrival in the Promised Land and the anointing of King Saul, the first king over Israel.

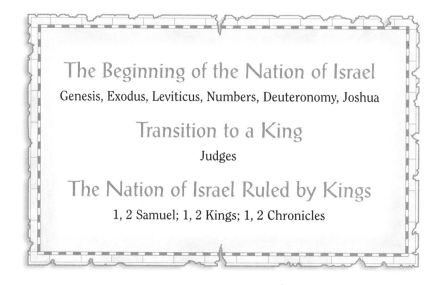

The Beginning of the Nation of Israel

Genesis, Exodus, Leviticus, Numbers, Deuteronomy, Joshua

Transition to a King

Judges

The Nation of Israel Ruled by Kings

1, 2 Samuel; 1, 2 Kings; 1, 2 Chronicles

Before their arrival in the Promised Land, the people of Israel were led by individual leaders such as Moses and Joshua. Moses, of course, was chosen by God to go to Pharaoh and demand that the Israelites be allowed to leave Egypt. It was Moses who led the nation out of Egypt, through the wilderness, and then he received the Ten Commandments from God. Joshua had the responsibility of leading the nation into the Promised Land. Now that the nation had arrived in this land, the Israelites were no longer led by a single leader. The twelve tribes of Israel settled in the portion of land given to each of them. This was now their home. The Israelites were to live according to God's principles as taught to them by Moses and Joshua. Their problems arose when they disobeyed.

Why Were There Judges?

Although the names and actions of the judges are important, it is even more important to understand why God "raised up" judges. In order to understand why there were judges, we need to review two very important passages of Scripture.

The first one is found in Deuteronomy 7:2: "And when the Lord your God delivers them over to you, you shall conquer them and utterly destroy them. You shall make no covenant with them nor show mercy to them." This command was supposed to be carried out by the people of Israel when they entered the land. They were commanded to do four things:

- smite their enemies
- utterly destroy their enemies
- make no covenant with their enemies
- show no mercy to their enemies.

Obviously, God did not want His chosen people to be corrupted by the pagans who were living in the Promised Land. Israel was to take over the land and drive out or totally destroy its inhabitants.

However, before the first chapter of Judges ends, we learn that the tribes of Israel did *not* drive out the inhabitants from the land. In the second chapter, after we are told about the death of Joshua, we read the following: "And they [the Israelites] forsook the Lord God of their fathers, who had brought them out of the land of Egypt; and they followed other gods from among the gods of the people who were all around them, and they bowed down to them; and they provoked the Lord to anger" (Judges 2:12).

As a result of their disobedience, God allowed the nation of Israel to be taken captive by its enemies. During each of the captivities described in the book of Judges, the people of Israel suffered.

After a period of suffering, the people would pray to God and ask Him to forgive them of their sins. Each time Israel prayed for forgiveness, God demonstrated His mercy by raising up a judge to deliver the people from their oppressors. Many times these judges conducted daring military campaigns to free the people. The book of Judges records the stories of each of the oppressions and the *Daring Deliverers* used by God to save the people.

These Judges Did Not Work in a Courtroom

If you have ever been in a courtroom, or seen a trial on television, you know what a judge does. A judge is someone who makes a decision when there is a dispute between two or more individuals. Although the word for judge is often used this way in the Bible, it is used in a very different way in the book of Judges.

During the period of the judges, the "judge" was an individual who "served as a leader." Although this leadership sometimes involved deciding cases, it also included serving in local government or as a military leader. The judges were ordinary people whom God empowered in a mighty way to lead His people during a period of oppression by an enemy nation. These judges served as leaders of the nation of Israel from the time the Israelites entered the Promised Land until the time Saul was anointed as king—a period of almost four hundred years!

BIBLE BACKGROUND

The Twelve Tribes of Israel

The nation of Israel consisted of twelve tribes, or families. The following is a list of these tribes with the meaning of each name noted in parentheses.

Judah (praise)	Dan (judge)
Manasseh (causing to forget)	Gad (troop)
Reuben (see, a son)	Issachar (man of hire)
Asher (happy)	Benjamin (son of my right hand)
Ephraim (fruitful)	Simeon (hearing)
Zebulun (dwelling)	Naphtali (my wrestling)

Do You Want to Be a Leader?

As you study each of the judges described throughout this course, you will learn that God punishes disobedience but also has mercy upon those who confess their sins. You will also learn about a period of Israel's history that includes some of the most well-known Bible stories ever told. But there is an added bonus available to you as you study this book. Since the judges were actual leaders, they have many important leadership lessons to teach us.

It is quite possible that you are already holding a position of leadership in your school. If not, maybe you would like to become a leader. Even though you may not hold a position of leadership right now, the chances are that someday you will.

Do you know what to do to prepare yourself to become a leader? One of the best ways you can prepare is to learn from the successes—and mistakes—of others! Throughout your study of the *Daring Deliverers* you will be taught many leadership lessons. From the lives of some of the judges you will learn effective leadership principles. These are the principles you will want to incorporate in your life. From the lives of other judges, you will learn about their mistakes. You will certainly want to avoid making these same mistakes! If you learn your lessons well, you will be ready when God calls you into service.

INCREASE YOUR UNDERSTANDING

1. Select two unfamiliar books, one each from the Old Testament and the New Testament, and explain why God included these books in the Bible.

2. Name a recent event in history that you believe demonstrates that God is in complete control of all that happens.

3. Why wasn't Moses allowed to enter the Promised Land with the Israelites?

4. The form of leadership God desired for Israel was a theocracy. What is a theocracy?

PREPARING FOR LEADERSHIP!

1. Israel's leaders were commanded to "drive out the inhabitants" of the land. Their disobedience brought God's judgment upon the nation. Select two important military leaders in our country's history. Why was absolute obedience necessary to their success as leaders?

2. In the book of Judges, the "judge" was an individual who "served as a leader." In your opinion, what does it mean to "serve as a leader"?

3. Of all the leaders living in the world today, which one do you admire most? What leadership characteristics are important to his or her success?

Chapter Two

Know Your Enemies!

Israel's Big Mistake

God was so good to the nation of Israel. In the days of Joseph, God protected the nation in a serious time of famine. When the Egyptian pharaohs decided to make slaves of the Israelites, God raised up Moses to lead them out of Egypt. When they arrived in the Promised Land, Joshua led them to victory over the inhabitants of the land. Every step of the way, God provided for His people.

However, God did give the Israelites a warning. They were to *totally occupy* this new land. They were not to share the land with any of the surrounding pagan nations. God knew that if they did, Israel would end up worshiping the pagan gods of these countries and marrying people who did not know the God of Israel.

While Joshua was still alive, the Israelites obeyed God. But after Joshua's death, the leaders of Israel were not as careful to heed God's warning. As time passed, the leaders of the various tribes began to make treaties with these pagan nations. God's warning to the Israelites was completely ignored. Their disobedience to God's clear commands would cause Israel to be oppressed by these nations for the next four centuries!

Who Were These Oppressors?

June 6, 1944, known as "D day," was a turning point in World War II. Under the command of General Dwight D. Eisenhower, the Allied troops landed on the beaches of Normandy in northwestern France. This began the long and difficult struggle to free France, as well as the rest of Europe, from Germany's control.

Although there were many uncertainties about the D-day invasion, at least one thing is known for sure. General Eisenhower and the rest of his commanders learned all they could about the enemy before preparing their plan of attack. Good military leaders always carefully study the enemy before staging an attack.

Because the Israelites did not obey God, He allowed other nations to rule over them. The oppressing nations appear in the book of Judges in the following order: Mesopotamia, Moab, Canaan, Midian, Ammon, and Philistia. For nearly four hundred years, these six nations brought severe punishment upon Israel. In order to understand how each of the judges delivered the nation of Israel from its oppressors, it is important to know something about the enemies.

The Mesopotamian Oppression

The word *mesopotamia* means "land between the rivers." Mesopotamia lies between the Tigris and Euphrates rivers, far to the north of the land of Israel. The people living in this region were well-educated and relatively wealthy. However, they were also known

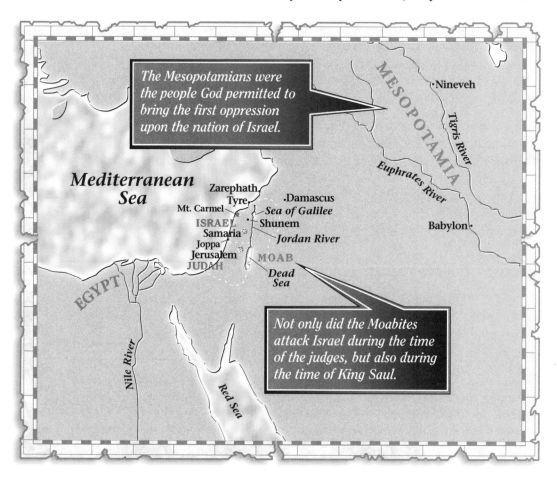

The Mesopotamians were the people God permitted to bring the first oppression upon the nation of Israel.

Not only did the Moabites attack Israel during the time of the judges, but also during the time of King Saul.

for their desire to conquer other cities. This is how they gained much of their wealth.

Mesopotamia is referred to frequently in the Bible. Abraham sent his servant to Nahor in Mesopotamia to find a bride for Isaac (Genesis 24:10). The pagan prophet, Balaam, came from Mesopotamia (Deuteronomy 23:4). When the Ammonites waged war against King David, they hired chariot and cavalry troops from Mesopotamia (1 Chronicles 19:6). Acts 2:9 refers to some of the Jews present at the Feast of Pentecost as "those dwelling in Mesopotamia."

The Mesopotamians were the people God permitted to bring the first oppression upon the nation of Israel. War and conquest was a way of life for the Mesopotamians. The nation was comprised of many well-trained, fierce soldiers who were unafraid of battle. They were experienced warriors who knew how to win.

The Moabite Oppression

The second nation to oppress Israel was Moab. While the Mesopotamians came from the far north, the Moabites lived just across the Dead Sea. The Israelite tribes of Reuben and Gad settled the northern part of the territory of Moab. During most of Israel's history, the Moabites were Israel's enemies. When it came time for them to attack Israel, they only had a few miles to travel.

The Moabites were named after Moab, a son of Lot who was born as a result of a sinful relationship between Lot and his eldest daughter. Since Lot was a nephew of Abraham, the Moabites were distant cousins of the Israelites. Because of the relationship, jealousy had always existed between the two nations. When the opportunity arose, the Moabites were quick to go to war against Israel.

Not only did the Moabites attack Israel during the time of the judges, but also during the time of King Saul. Both Judge Ehud and King Saul were successful in controlling them. However, it was during David's reign that the Moabites were completely conquered. The Moabites remained under Israel's control until after the death of Solomon.

The Canaanite Oppression

The third oppression came from the Canaanites, who had lived in the land of Palestine even before the Israelites arrived. The Canaanites were a highly civilized people.

These are the same people that the Israelites should have driven from the land when they first arrived. Since the Canaanites lost many previous battles with Israel, they were still very angry about the land they had lost. They were certainly ready for revenge.

The Canaanites could be considered the most religious of all of the enemy nations. However, their religion featured many gods. These gods were worshiped with elaborate rituals. Various kinds of priests officiated at these pagan ceremonies. Their religious system also

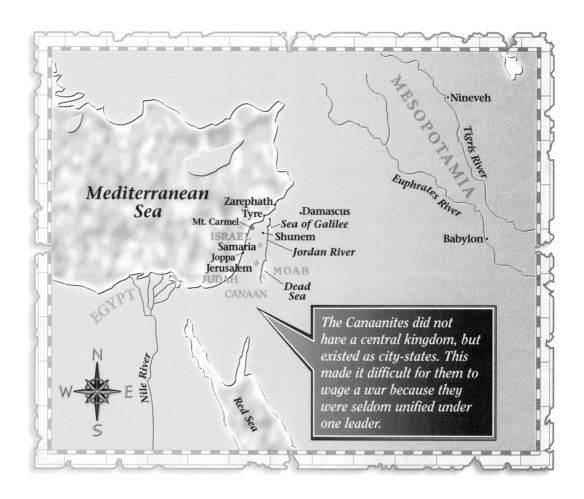

The Canaanites did not have a central kingdom, but existed as city-states. This made it difficult for them to wage a war because they were seldom unified under one leader.

featured many different types of worship, from simple outdoor altars to massive stone temples.

The Canaanites did not have a central kingdom, but existed as city-states. This made it difficult for them to wage a war because they were seldom unified under one leader. However, during the time of the Canaanite oppression, they were much more organized than they had been in previous years.

The Midianite Oppression

The Midianites were a nomadic people who were enemies of the Israelites throughout the Old Testament. The Midianites were also related to the Israelites, since they sprang from Midian, one of the sons of Abraham.

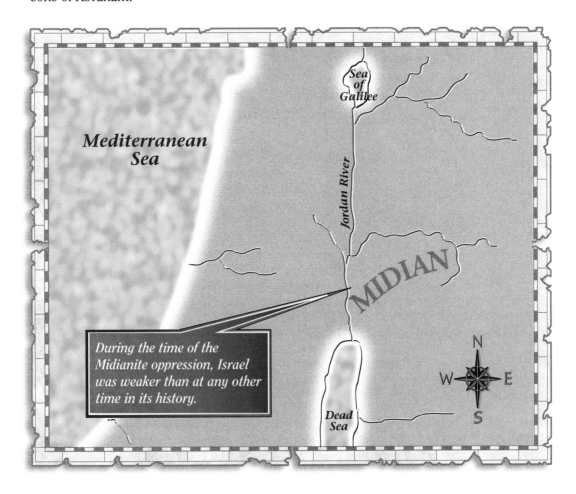

During the time of the Midianite oppression, Israel was weaker than at any other time in its history.

The Midianites were assisted by other groups of people when they attacked Israel. The way in which the Midianites oppressed Israel was very humiliating. They did not enter the land of Israel and set up a central place of authority to rule the nation on a day-to-day basis. They invaded only once each year—at the time of harvest—to take the freshly harvested crops. The people of Israel would labor all year to grow a good crop only to have it stolen from them by the Midianites right after the harvest.

During this entire oppression, there was no attempt by Israel to fight back. The Midianites simply came, took what they wanted, stayed as long as they wished, and then left when they felt like it. During the time of the Midianite oppression, Israel was weaker than at any other time in its history.

The Ammonite Oppression

Up until this time, the four previous oppressions had not caused the nation of Israel to change its sinful ways. As a matter of fact, Israel's sin had increased. It was only with the last two oppressions, the Ammonites and the Philistines, that the Israelites were finally willing to change their behavior.

The Ammonites were also a nomadic race, descended from another of Lot's sons, Ammon. During the days of the Exodus, the Israelites were instructed by God not to associate with the Ammonites (Deuteronomy 23:3). No reason is given in the Bible for such hostility, but there was obviously a great tension between the two nations.

The Ammonites were a very strong people. However, before Israel, they had to defeat Moab and Midian. This was accomplished without much difficulty. At first, the Ammonites attacked only those tribes on the east of the river Jordan. Once they set up border fortresses for protection, they moved out to possess the rest of the land.

The Philistine Oppression

The sixth and last great oppression was brought by the Philistines. Called the "Sea People" by the Egyptians because of their ability to wage a war from the sea, the Philistines always had a warlike tradition. They controlled Israel for forty years—the longest of any of the oppressors.

The Philistines dominated the entire land of Israel. They possessed superior weapons of iron. Since the Israelites did not have the capability to obtain or work with iron, this was a great advantage for the Philistines when they prepared to wage war.

It was the threat of the Philistines that prompted Israel to ask for a king. Israel believed that a king would be able to protect them from the Philistines. However, even under King Saul, the nation was threatened by the Philistines. This threat ultimately resulted in Saul's death. When David slew Goliath, the Philistine giant from the city of Gath, he was immediately proclaimed a hero. The Israelites were very afraid of the Philistines and were looking for anyone who could provide protection from these ruthless warriors.

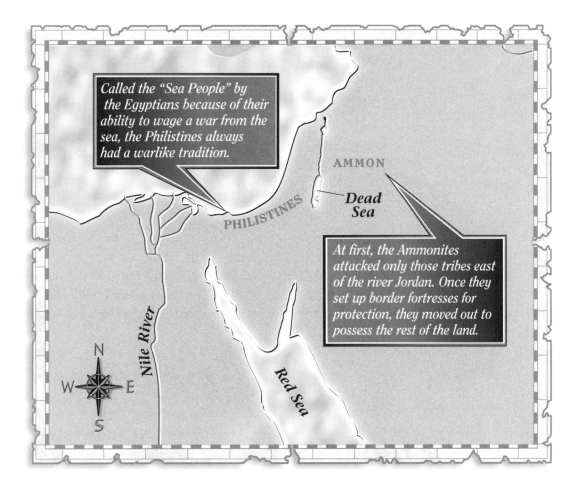

Let the Story Begin!

Now that you have been introduced to the period of the judges and a brief description of each of the oppressing nations, it is time to begin our study of these *Daring Deliverers*. The stories recorded in the book of Judges are unlike any you have ever read. The judges were average people who were empowered by God to rescue the nation of Israel from its enemies.

But the story surrounding each of these *Daring Deliverers* is not the only focus of our study. We will also consider the leadership lessons that we can learn from each judge. Do you want to be a leader? If so, these *Daring Deliverers* have a lot to teach you.

INCREASE YOUR UNDERSTANDING

1. Prepare a brief summary of the D-day invasion. If possible, interview a soldier who fought in World War II to learn about the importance of this invasion.

2. Why do you think Israel had so many enemies?

3. The Moabites and Ammonites were descendents of Moab and Ammon, sons of Lot. What do you know about Lot's influence on his family that helps you understand why these two nations acted the way that they did?

PREPARING FOR LEADERSHIP!

Our country has fought in a number of wars in the last one hundred years. Four wars are noted on the following chart. Conduct brief research on each of these wars. Begin by noting the oppressors for each war. Then identify a major military leader for each war and an important leadership lesson that you can learn from this leader's life.

War	Oppressors	Military Leader	Leadership Lesson
World War I			
World War II			
Korean War			
Vietnam War			

CHAPTER THREE

Othniel

A Man Who Was Ready and Able

(Judges 3:7–11)

Israel's Merry-Go-Round

County and state fairs have what they call the "midway"—a special area that has many carnival rides. Little children like to ride on the various cars, planes, fire engines, and boats. All these rides have one thing in common: they end up right where they started. After you get off the ride, you really haven't gone anywhere.

Jim was like many little children. He was anxious to ride on the merry-go-round. He paid his money and hopped on the nearest horse. After a few minutes, the ride slowly came to an end. When he got off, he realized that he was at the same spot where he had gotten on. With his small arms, he measured the distance—about a yard. "It wasn't worth the money, Dad," he said. "I only went three feet."

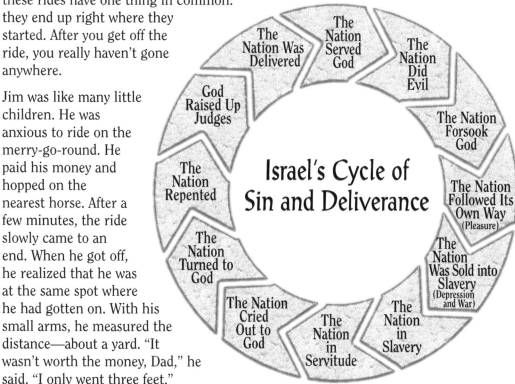

Israel's Cycle of Sin and Deliverance

The Nation Served God
The Nation Did Evil
The Nation Forsook God
The Nation Followed Its Own Way (Pleasure)
The Nation Was Sold into Slavery (Depression and War)
The Nation in Slavery
The Nation in Servitude
The Nation Cried Out to God
The Nation Turned to God
The Nation Repented
God Raised Up Judges
The Nation Was Delivered

The expression "going around in circles" could apply to the twelve tribes of Israel during the four hundred years described in the book of Judges. Israel's pattern of behavior followed a very predictable cycle: sin; God gave the Israelites over to heathen nations; oppression; Israel cried out to the Lord; God heard and raised up a judge; Israel was true to God while the judge lived; the nation returned to sin and the cycle started all over again.

In Judges 3, we are introduced to Othniel, the first of the twelve *Daring Deliverers*. He was a man mightily used by God in a very difficult situation. As you study the story surrounding the life of Othniel, you will be introduced to Israel's cycle of sin and deliverance rather quickly.

The Attack of Cushan-Rishathaim

For a number of years the nation of Israel and the Canaanites lived side by side in Palestine. As each year passed, the Israelites became

"The children of Israel served Cushan-Rishathaim eight years" (Judges 3:8).

more used to the pagan gods and practices of their neighbors. No longer did the nation of Israel only serve the true and living God. In order to be like their neighbors, the people participated in many of the pagan rituals. Finally, Israel's sins were more than God would tolerate. Because the nation disobeyed Him, He delivered the Israelites into the hands of their enemy, Mesopotamia.

The armies of Mesopotamia had been active in the north for a number of years. Under the leadership of Cushan-Rishathaim, the Mesopotamians went to war against the Canaanites. The Canaanites were no match for the strong Mesopotamian army and were quickly defeated. Once victory over the Canaanites had been achieved, Cushan-Rishathaim turned his attention to the nation of Israel. Israel, unprepared for war, was easily defeated.

The Bible says that "the children of Israel served Cushan-Rishathaim eight years" (Judges 3:8). The Mesopotamians were strong and mighty warriors. The Israelites were soon under the complete control of Cushan-Rishathaim and his army. During these eight years, the Mesopotamians extended their control throughout all the land of Israel. As each year passed, the suffering of the Israelites increased. Finally Israel cried out to the Lord for help. Othniel was chosen to deliver the nation from the hands of the Mesopotamians.

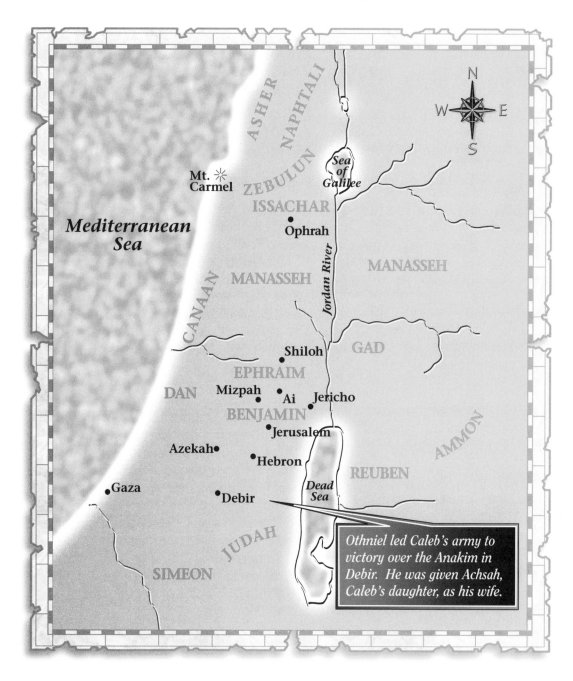

Othniel led Caleb's army to victory over the Anakim in Debir. He was given Achsah, Caleb's daughter, as his wife.

Othniel Had Previous Battle Experience

Although we are told very little about Othniel in the book of Judges, we learn much about him from the book of Joshua. Beginning in Joshua 14, we learn that Caleb was Othniel's uncle. It seemed that Caleb had been granted an area of land that was occupied by a group of people known as the Anakim. Caleb defeated the Anakim in the area surrounding the city of Hebron and took possession of the land. However, the Anakim still controlled the area surrounding the city of Debir.

Caleb asked for a volunteer to lead his army against the Anakim in Debir. Caleb promised his daughter, Achsah, as wife to the one who would successfully defeat the Anakim. Othniel volunteered, led the army to victory, and was given Achsah as his wife. At the time of his victory, Othniel was probably about nineteen years old. Although Othniel was only a teenager, he demonstrated his ability as a soldier and as a leader.

Othniel Gains Victory over Cushan-Rishathaim

Thirty years later, God called upon Othniel to lead an army against Cushan-Rishathaim and the Mesopotamians. Nearly fifty years old, Othniel was no longer a young man. The story of Othniel's victory over the enemy is very brief. It states merely that "he went out to war, and the Lord delivered Cushan-Rishathaim king of Mesopotamia into his hand" (Judges 3:10). Although we are not given many details about the actual events surrounding the battle, there are a number of things that we know must be true.

BIBLE BACKGROUND

Characteristics of War in the Old Testament

War, during Old Testament times, was carried out by soldiers in hand-to-hand combat. Very few nations had the luxury of horses and chariots. Body armor, swords, and bows were the typical weapons of the day.

Although the majority of battles took place in an open field, conquering the major cities of one's enemy was also an important focus of the battle.

Besieging a city required elaborate planning. If possible, the city's water supply was cut off. Often the towers and gates of the city were set on fire. In order for armies to use their battering rams and catapults to propel arrows or stones, mounds were built to raise the weapons to appropriate heights. Scaling ladders were laid against the wall so soldiers could get inside the city.

First, Othniel would have to raise up an army. There had not been an army in Israel since the time of Joshua. Since Othniel had settled in the area of Debir, he probably gathered his troops from that area.

Second, he would have to train these troops. More than likely, the men he gathered for his army were individuals who had never before been in battle. They were not accustomed to the hardships of war. This training would also have been done in secrecy. The Mesopotamians controlled the land. They had troops stationed in all of the cities, including Debir. Certainly a large group of men, gathering together for any reason, would cause suspicion. Othniel needed to be careful when and where he trained his troops.

"In contrast, Othniel's troops could best be characterized as farmers and sheepherders."

Finally, Othniel was going into battle against experienced and skilled warriors. The Mesopotamian troops had been in countless battles for many years. Their knowledge of battle strategy and the quality of their weapons would have been the best available. They were used to winning and then taking control of everything in sight.

In contrast, Othniel's troops could best be characterized as farmers and sheepherders. They were peaceful men, who lived with their families and took care of their land. From all outward appearances, it looked as if Cushan-Rishathaim would "walk away" with an easy victory!

Under God's blessing, however, Othniel's army came through with a decisive victory and the enemy was driven from the land. The Bible records that after the defeat of Cushan-Rishathaim, "the land had rest forty years" (Judges 3:11). This means that forty years elapsed before the second oppression, brought by the Moabites, was permitted by God. Othniel was a strong leader in this crucial situation. Although he did not lead any more troops into battle in the next forty years, he certainly provided leadership to his people.

COURAGE

Othniel's Lesson on Leadership!

When we study the Bible, we must remember that God is not only providing us with historical information but also with matters of spiritual truth which can serve as lessons to Christians in any generation. Although there are many important lessons that we can learn from all of the judges in this series, we will focus on one particular *Lesson on Leadership!* for each of them.

One of the obvious leadership characteristics of Othniel was his courage. He was willing to attempt difficult and dangerous assignments for God. This was first shown when he volunteered to fight the fearsome Anakim near Debir. These were giant people who had caused fear to ten of the twelve spies who reported at Kadesh Barnea years before (Numbers 13:32, 33). Even though Othniel was only a teenager, he was not afraid to lead Caleb's troops into battle.

Othniel also showed remarkable courage when he was selected by God to deliver Israel from the powerful Mesopotamians. Although he was confident that God would bring victory, there were certainly others who did not share his confidence. Nevertheless, he raised up an army, trained them in secrecy, and then led them to victory over the enemy. Even though he was not a young man, he once again demonstrated the courage necessary to lead others.

God is looking for courageous leaders today. Courage is not a characteristic that is only displayed on the battlefield. Courage begins by doing what you know is right, in spite of what everyone else thinks. God is looking for those who will be obedient to His Word and trust Him for the victory, no matter how discouraging the situation might be.

1. Using a Bible dictionary, prepare a brief biographical sketch of Cushan-Rishathaim, the Mesopotamian leader.

2. Draw "Israel's Cycle of Sin and Deliverance" on a sheet of plain paper. From the first three chapters of Judges, note the verse(s) that correspond to each description noted on the cycle.

PREPARING FOR LEADERSHIP!

1. As he was gathering troops for his army, Othniel had to convince them why they should follow him. Leaders always have to demonstrate why they should be trusted. In your opinion, what reasons do you think Othniel gave to his soldiers as to why they should follow him? What reasons would you give others as to why they should follow you?

2. Name a leader that you admire for his or her courage. Explain how this courage has contributed to this leader's success.

3. How have you demonstrated courage in decisions you have made? What specific steps can you take to ensure that you will be a courageous leader?

CHAPTER FOUR

Ehud

Going One-on-One with the King

(Judges 3:12–30)

The Cycle of Sin and Deliverance Continues

"And the children of Israel again did evil in the sight of the Lord. So the Lord strengthened Eglon king of Moab against Israel, because they had done evil in the sight of the Lord" (Judges 3:12). Did you notice the word *again* in this verse? God is reminding us that the nation of Israel was continuing in its cycle of sin and deliverance: sin, oppression, deliverance, faithfulness to God, and return to sin. The Israelites forgot the deliverance that Othniel led just forty years before and once again returned to their wicked ways.

The story of Ehud and King Eglon is one of the most fascinating stories in the Bible. Going one-on-one with the king is obviously not referring to a basketball game. Although leading an army against the enemy was the common battle strategy, it was not Ehud's approach. Ehud acted alone to deliver Israel from the hands of the Moabites. His battle strategy, leading ultimately to victory over the Moabites, is unique to the entire book of Judges.

Who Were These Moabites?

It had been almost eighty years since Moab and Israel confronted one another. In Numbers 22–24, we are told that the Moabite king, Balak, considered the nation of Israel a menace and wished to destroy it. In order to ensure that the nation would suffer defeat, Balak brought the sorcerer Balaam to pronounce a curse on Israel. But Balaam was restricted by God from obeying the Moabite king.

BIBLE BACKGROUND

The Prophet Balaam

Balaam was a magician (Joshua 13:22) who was summoned by the Moabite king Balak to curse the Israelites before they entered Canaan (Numbers 22:5–24:25). At first, Balaam did not want to go with the king's messengers to perform this curse. But he finally agreed to go when the Lord specifically told him to do so (Numbers 22:20).

While Balaam was on his way to see Balak, the angel of the Lord told him that he was only to speak the words God gave him to speak. When Balaam finally met King Balak, they offered sacrifices to the pagan gods. Balaam then went off by himself. It was during this time that God told Balaam to bless the people that Balak wanted him to curse. Balaam returned and did as God had commanded him.

However, before leaving Balak, Balaam told the Moabite leader that Israel could be defeated if its people were encouraged to worship Baal. According to Numbers 25:1–3, this is exactly what happened: "Then Israel remained in Acacia Grove, and the people began to commit harlotry with the women of Moab. They invited the people to the sacrifices of their gods, and the people ate and bowed down to their gods. So Israel was joined to Baal of Peor, and the anger of the Lord was aroused against Israel."

Balaam is condemned in the New Testament (2 Peter 2:15; Jude 11; Revelation 2:14) because he tempted God's people to compromise their moral standards and worship a pagan god.

Finally, however, the prophet did assist Moab by enticing the Israelite men to take part in pagan worship. As a result of this action, God sent Moses and an army of twelve thousand to punish Moab and kill Balaam.

For the past eighty years, Israel and Moab had not been on very friendly terms. During this time, Moab continued to gain power by defeating such nations as the Ammonites and Amalekites. Thus when the opportunity arose to attack Israel, Moab jumped at the chance.

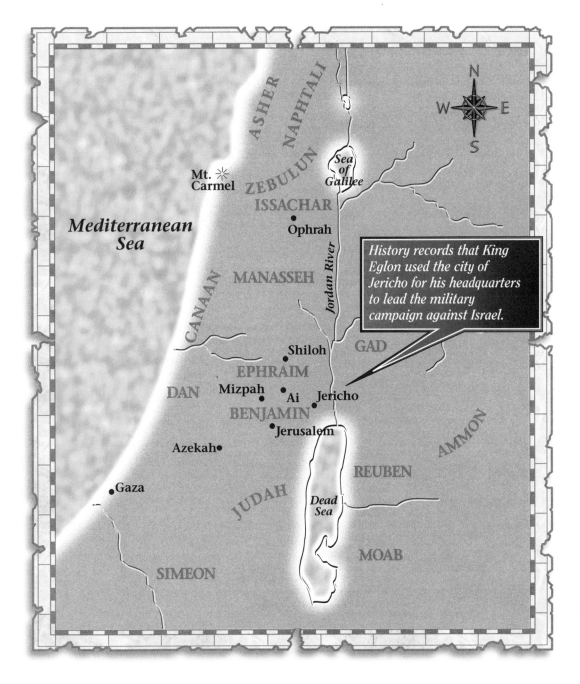

ASHER

NAPHTALI

Sea of Galilee

Mt. Carmel

ZEBULUN

ISSACHAR

Ophrah

Mediterranean Sea

CANAAN

MANASSEH

Jordan River

History records that King Eglon used the city of Jericho for his headquarters to lead the military campaign against Israel.

Shiloh

GAD

EPHRAIM

DAN

Mizpah

Ai

Jericho

BENJAMIN

Jerusalem

Azekah

AMMON

REUBEN

Gaza

JUDAH

Dead Sea

MOAB

SIMEON

History records that King Eglon used the city of Jericho for his headquarters to lead the military campaign against Israel. Jericho had been desolate ever since Joshua destroyed it during the time of the conquest of the Promised Land. As a matter of fact, Joshua placed a curse on whoever should try to rebuild the city (Joshua 6:26). We do not know whether or not King Eglon knew about the curse. Because Jericho was centrally located, it became his fortress for controlling all of the cities of Israel.

Ehud—His Strategy for Victory

The person whom God raised up to bring deliverance from the Moabites was Ehud, of the tribe of Benjamin. Evidently, Ehud was already in a position of authority for he was assigned the task of bringing tribute (a present) to King Eglon. This was probably an annual tribute that the Moabites required from Israel. In exchange for the tribute, the Moabites would promise not to attack Israel.

Tribute paying was customary in such situations, and it was normally required that the person bringing it be important among his people. The king who imposed the tribute was made to feel more important when a leader was forced to humble himself by personally bringing the gift.

Not only does the Bible describe the tribute demanded by King Eglon, it also notes a unique characteristic of the one who was bringing it. The Bible says that Ehud was left-handed. It is very unusual for the Bible to identify whether a person is right- or left-handed. However, the fact that Ehud was left-handed is very important to the rest of the story.

Since Ehud was assigned to head this tribute-bearing mission, he planned to take advantage of this private meeting to make a personal attack on the king. He hid a dagger, apparently of his own making (Judges 3:16), under his clothing on the right side where he could grasp it easily with his left hand. It was a rare type of dagger, only one cubit (eighteen inches) long and double-edged. It had to be short to be easily hidden, and being hidden on his right side, it was less detectable. Since most people are right-handed, the king's guards would have been looking for a weapon on Ehud's left side.

Ehud and his companions went to the palace of King Eglon to deliver the tribute. Ehud left the palace with his group to return home. But as he approached Gilgal after delivering the gift, he abruptly left the others and returned to the king's palace alone. It was now time for the most daring part of his mission.

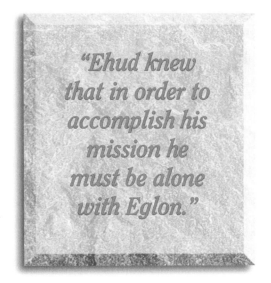

"Ehud knew that in order to accomplish his mission he must be alone with Eglon."

Ehud requested that the king dismiss everyone who was in the room. He based his request upon the fact that he had a secret message for the king that no one else could hear. Ehud knew that in order to accomplish his mission he must be alone with Eglon.

King Eglon was quite curious when Ehud said he had a secret message. He dismissed his servants and invited Ehud to join him in the summer parlor where they could be alone and Ehud could tell him the secret. The summer parlor was probably a room at the top of the palace where the king would go for privacy.

Ehud was now completely alone with the king. He drew closer to Eglon, as if to deliver his secret message. All of a sudden he drew the dagger from his right thigh with his left hand and plunged it into the king's midsection. The Bible records that King Eglon was such a fat man that the fat closed over the weapon so that Ehud was unable to pull it out. Ehud had no choice but to leave the knife in the belly of the king.

Once he knew that the enemy ruler was dead, Ehud calmly left the room. As he went out the door, he locked it behind him. According to the Bible, he was able to leave without being noticed by the guards.

Later on, Eglon's servants became concerned that they had not heard from their king. Since the door was locked, they were afraid to disturb him. Because of their delay, Ehud had plenty of time to make his escape. Finally, the guards could wait no longer. They pried open the door—only to find their king lying dead on the floor.

Next Comes the Battle!

Ehud hurried to the hill country of Ephraim to gather his troops together for battle against the Moabites. The first thing he needed to do was control the crossing points along the river Jordan. If he failed to control these places, the Moabites could return to their home country and recruit additional warriors.

The Bible records that Ehud and his troops were totally successful. They took control of the crossing points and killed nearly ten thousand Moabites who were trying to return home. The loss of their king and ten thousand warriors left the nation of Moab weak and unable to retaliate.

This ended the Moabite oppression. After Ehud's victory, the nation of Israel enjoyed an eighty-year period of peace, the longest of any period during the time of the judges (Judges 3:30). Although Ehud did not serve as judge throughout this entire eighty-year period, we do know that he provided leadership to the nation for at least part of that time.

LESSONS ON LEADERSHIP!

WILLINGNESS TO STAND ALONE

Ehud's Lesson on Leadership!

Stop for a moment and think about what it must have been like for Ehud to return to the palace of King Eglon all alone. Although he had a very good plan, Ehud had no idea if it would really work. There were so many things that could go wrong. What if King Eglon did not dismiss his servants to hear the secret? Would the king cry out in pain when stabbed with the dagger? What would Ehud do if Eglon's servants entered the king's room before he had escaped from the palace? What if he and his troops could not stop the Moabite soldiers from returning to Moab to recruit more troops?

The Bible indicates that Ehud tried to solicit the help of others in his plan to kill the king, but no one was willing to help. Since no one was willing to take the risk with him, Ehud realized that he would have to work alone. Although it was very dangerous, Ehud carried out his mission perfectly.

Sometimes leaders must be willing to stand alone. It is always easier to lead when others agree with you and support what you are doing. But that will not always happen. There will be times when your decisions will be opposed. When you are confident that God desires for you to make a specific leadership decision, then you must be obedient to Him.

Ehud was confident that God would give him victory over King Eglon and the Moabites. Ehud's responsibility was to be obedient to God, even if it meant standing all alone. Because of his leadership, Israel was delivered from Moab and experienced the longest period of peace recorded in the book of Judges.

INCREASE YOUR UNDERSTANDING

1. Research the responsibilities of a prophet in the Old Testament. Explain how the prophet Balaam failed to fulfill his responsibilities.

2. Give other examples, from both the Old and New Testaments, of individuals bringing tributes (gifts) to a king.

3. Conduct an interview with your principal, pastor, or another church leader. Discuss times when this leader had to make an unpopular decision and stand alone for what he or she knew was the right thing to do. Ask for some guidelines that could help you stand firm when you are faced with a difficult and unpopular decision.

PREPARING FOR LEADERSHIP!

1. Talk with your pastor or youth leader about leadership principles. Write down his or her comments about what it means to be an effective, godly leader.

2. Have you ever had to stand alone for what you believe? If so, describe what happened.

CHAPTER FIVE

Shamgar
Parenthetical But Powerful
(Judges 3:31)

Have you ever written a story or a letter to someone and put some of your comments in parentheses? For example:

> *Dear Jason,*
>
> *I'm sorry that you could not attend the football game with us today. It was a great game (although it kept us on the edge of our seats for over four hours). Our team rallied to win by kicking a field goal on the final play of the game. I hope you can go with us next week.*
>
> *Your friend,*
>
> *Ben*

Ben's comments about the length of the game were placed in parentheses because they helped the reader better understand the main purpose for writing the letter. That is, to tell Jason how good the football game was. Ben's parenthetical comments provided additional information to further support his statement that it was a "great game."

Many Bible scholars believe that the story of Shamgar, because it is only one verse in length (Judges 3:31), is a parenthetical comment. Many believe that the verse could have been put in parentheses as follows: "(After him was Shamgar the son of Anath, who killed six hundred men of the Philistines with an ox goad; and he also delivered Israel.)"

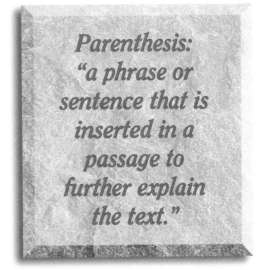

Parenthesis: "a phrase or sentence that is inserted in a passage to further explain the text."

The story of Shamgar's deliverance is the briefest of any judge. However, it once again reminds us that the nation of Israel was still being terrorized by other nations. Although the battle did not involve a large number (only six hundred Philistines), the conflict did indicate that the eighty-year period of peace, resulting from Ehud's victory, was coming to an end.

The First of the Minor Judges

Even though the Bible does not place the judges into the categories of "major" or "minor," Bible scholars have done so in order to better organize the events recorded in the book of Judges. Shamgar is the first of the six "minor" judges. Although six of the judges are classified as minor, it does not mean that their work was unimportant. A judge was classified as minor for the following reasons:

- the judge did not lead a military deliverance
- a limited amount of space in the Biblical text was devoted to the judge's story.

Certainly, Shamgar meets these two criteria for a minor judge. He did not lead a military force against the Philistines. As a matter of fact, he killed the six hundred Philistines all by himself. Also, his story is told in only one verse. This is the shortest record for any of the minor judges.

Major Judges	Minor Judges
Othniel	Shamgar
Ehud	Tola
Deborah	Jair
Gideon	Ibzan
Jephthah	Elon
Samson	Abdon
Samuel	

How Important Was Shamgar?

Since only one verse was devoted to Shamgar's story, it would be easy to assume that even what he did as a minor judge was unimportant. However, just the opposite is true. Shamgar was included in the book of Judges because his story was too important to be omitted.

The account of his deliverance occurs between the stories of two of the major judges, Ehud and Deborah. His attack on the Philistines indicated that the eighty-year period of peace that began with Ehud's victory was quickly coming to an end. His willingness to single-handedly fight six hundred Philistines demonstrated that the Israelites were under severe oppression and that a major deliverance was needed. This, of course, would happen under the next major judge, Deborah.

The story of Shamgar is also important because it demonstrates that the oppression in Israel had become so serious that even common men, such as Shamgar, were willing to risk their lives to control the Philistines. Although the account of his deliverance was only parenthetical, the message he sent to the Philistines was powerful!

His Slaughter of Six Hundred Philistines

Even though the Philistines were already powerful enough to cause Israel serious problems, they would become much more powerful by the time of Samson. The Philistines were a people who thrived on war and conquest. It was their intent to control all of Israel. At the time of Shamgar, they had begun to enter the Promised Land and conquer selected cities. These cities would be used as fortresses where Philistine soldiers would live while they conducted raids throughout the countryside. They tortured their captives and destroyed everything in sight.

When Bible students first read the story of Shamgar they ask, "How was Shamgar able to kill so many people all by himself?" Since no details are given, other than the mention of the "ox goad," we can only speculate as to what actually happened.

Did the total slaughter take place all at once or could it have taken place over time? All the Bible says is that he "killed six hundred men of the Philistines." Nothing is said as to how long it took him to do so. It is quite possible that Shamgar conducted guerrilla warfare against the Philistines over a long period.

The ox goad was certainly not the normal weapon used in battle. Sometimes the ox goad is confused with the "jawbone of a donkey" used by Samson to kill the Philistines. Although these were both very unusual weapons, they were also very different.

The ox goad was a more dangerous weapon than a jawbone. It was sometimes as much as eight feet long and six inches in circumference at the thick end. It was sharpened at the other end so that it could be used to prod and drive oxen. Made of hard wood, it would be a powerful weapon in the hands of a strong man such as Shamgar. It is even possible that Shamgar deliberately chose this unusual type of weapon because of the element of surprise. A group of Philistines would not expect to be attacked by a man with an ox goad.

Of course, it is important to realize that Shamgar did not gain the victory over the Philistines in his own strength. It was God who gave him the power and wisdom to defeat the Philistines.

It would be interesting to know how Shamgar went about the task of slaying the six hundred Philistines and how much planning he did beforehand. But what is important is that he was successful in defeating the Philistines and providing relief to the Israelites in the area. Shamgar's name may not be listed in the *Who's Who* of military generals, but to those who lived in his hometown, he was certainly a *Daring Deliverer!*

LESSONS ON LEADERSHIP!

ABILITY DEVOTED TO GOD'S SERVICE

Shamgar's Lesson on Leadership!

In order for Shamgar to single-handedly defeat six hundred Philistines with an ox goad, he must have been a very large and powerful man. But, of course, he possessed more than just physical strength. The ability to kill that many men without getting caught required intelligence and careful planning. It also took a lot of courage to do what he did.

Shamgar clearly demonstrated an important *Lesson on Leadership!*: "The abilities that God has given to us should be used for His service." Shamgar's strength, intelligence, and courage were given to him by God. He could have used these abilities to provide greater personal security for himself and his family. Or he could have used these abilities to increase his wealth or authority over others.

Shamgar did not use his God-given abilities for personal benefit. He used them to help and protect God's people.

This is an important lesson for those who desire to be godly leaders. The Bible reminds us that we are to be good stewards of the gifts God has given to us. The parable of the talents (Luke 19:12–27) reminds us that God holds us accountable. An important question for each of us to ask is "Am I using my God-given abilities for His service?"

THE PARABLE OF THE TALENTS

Luke 19:12–27

Therefore He said:

A certain nobleman went into a far country to receive for himself a kingdom and to return. So he called ten of his servants, delivered to them ten minas, and said to them, "Do business till I come."

But his citizens hated him, and sent a delegation after him, saying, "We will not have this man to reign over us."

And so it was that when he returned, having received the kingdom, he then commanded these servants, to whom he had given the money, to be called to him, that he might know how much every man had gained by trading.

Then came the first, saying, "Master, your mina has earned ten minas."

And he said to him, "Well done, good servant; because you were faithful in a very little, have authority over ten cities."

And the second came, saying, "Master, your mina has earned five minas."

Likewise he said to him, "You also be over five cities."

And another came, saying, "Master, here is your mina, which I have kept put away in a handkerchief. For I feared you, because you are an austere man. You collect what you did not deposit, and reap what you did not sow."

And he said to him, "Out of your own mouth I will judge you, you wicked servant. You knew that I was an austere man, collecting what I did not deposit and reaping what I did not sow.

"Why then did you not put my money in the bank, that at my coming I might have collected it with interest?"

And he said to those who stood by, "Take the mina from him, and give it to him who has ten minas."

(But they said to him, "Master, he has ten minas.")

"For I say to you, that to everyone who has will be given; and from him who does not have, even what he has will be taken away from him.

"But bring here those enemies of mine, who did not want me to reign over them, and slay them before me."

1. Prepare a brief report on the characteristics of guerrilla warfare. Note how guerrilla warfare has been used in recent wars. Identify the characteristics of guerrilla warfare that Shamgar could have used against the Philistines.

2. Jesus used parables to teach His followers spiritual truths. Select three of Jesus' parables and identify the spiritual lesson in each. Give a specific example of how each of these lessons is important to your daily life.

PREPARING FOR LEADERSHIP!

Make a list of the special abilities that God has given to you before answering the following questions:

1. How do you know you have these abilities?

2. In what ways are you presently using these abilities for God's glory?

3. As you think about the next ten years of your life, how do you think you might use these abilities for future service to Him?

CHAPTER SIX

Deborah
Two Women and a War
(Judges 4, 5)

On a popular television program some years ago, a contestant was asked the "big" question which was worth several thousand dollars: "Name the Old Testament woman who killed a captain by piercing his temple with a spike!" The contestant, familiar with God's Word, immediately gave the answer "Jael." The master of ceremonies wasn't sure she was right and had to turn to the experts for verification. The judges confirmed that Jael was indeed the answer.

If you had been asked this question, would you have known the answer? The story of Deborah, which includes the account of Jael and Sisera, is one of the most fascinating stories in the Bible. Deborah and Jael are among the many women in the Bible that God used in a mighty way to accomplish His purposes.

Punishment at the Hands of the Canaanites

Once again the children of Israel were on the merry-go-round of sin. After Ehud died, "the children of Israel again did evil in the sight of the Lord" (Judges 4:1). After all the good years under Ehud's leadership, the children of Israel failed to learn that God blesses obedience and punishes disobedience.

This time the Lord allowed Israel to be oppressed by the Canaanites. At the time of the Canaanite oppression, Jabin was the nation's king. He was a powerful king who had a mighty captain named Sisera. These two men inflicted terrible pain upon the people of Israel.

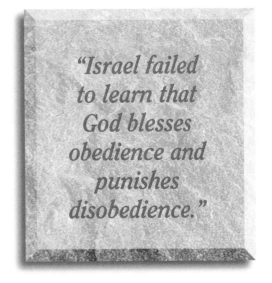

"Israel failed to learn that God blesses obedience and punishes disobedience."

When Israel first entered the Promised Land, the Canaanites were clearly in control. However, under Joshua's leadership, the Canaanites were driven from the land. At the time of Joshua's conquest, the Canaanites existed as city-states rather than as a centralized kingdom. This hurt them because they were unable to wage a unified and centralized war against Joshua and his army.

However, times had changed since Israel's early conquest of the Canaanites. Although they still existed as city-states, the Canaanites were now well organized under King Jabin. His success was due—in large part—to his military commander, Sisera.

Sisera had under his command as many as nine hundred chariots of iron. The mention of the chariots of iron (Judges 4:3) was an indication of the wealth and power of the Canaanites. In order to make chariots of iron, a nation would need many skilled laborers and great wealth. Producing iron was a very expensive process. In addition to the chariots, the Canaanites also had hundreds of horses. The possession of horses was another indication of the wealth and power of the Canaanites.

However, Sisera's army consisted of more than the nine hundred chariots of iron. In addition to the hundreds of soldiers necessary to drive the chariots, thousands of foot soldiers were also needed to wage war in the areas where chariots could not be driven. The Canaanites had amassed an incredible army. The Israelites had every reason to be afraid.

Introducing Deborah and Barak

In Judges 4:4–9 we learn about Deborah, the woman that the Lord used to deliver Israel from the Canaanites. Deborah is unique for a number of reasons. Not only is she the only woman judge, she is also described as a prophetess. She certainly had to be a brilliant and capable woman to hold such important positions of leadership.

Whereas Deborah lived between Ramah and Bethel, Barak lived at Kedesh of Naphtali. That is important to note because Deborah did not live in the area of the oppression while Barak lived right in the middle of it.

The Bible does not tell us exactly why Deborah chose Barak as her military leader. It is clear that she realized the task of military leadership was not for her, a woman. Since she was serving in a position of leadership in Israel, she must have heard about the military abilities of Barak. He was probably a natural choice because he was a successful military leader who lived in the actual area in which the Canaanites were the strongest.

Preparation for the Battle

Deborah sent for Barak. Her first message to him outlined the task and his responsibilities. Barak responded that he would accept the task, but only if Deborah worked with him. As a result of his dependence upon her, she told Barak that a woman would receive the honor of slaying the Canaanite military leader, Sisera. Of course, as we learn from Judges 4:18–22 and 5:24–27, she was not referring to herself but to a woman named Jael.

From this point on, Deborah and Barak worked together. They returned to Barak's home country and recruited ten thousand troops for the upcoming battle. They then led the troops to Mt. Tabor, in the Esdraelon Plain, to prepare for the battle. Sisera, the Canaanite general, was in the plain with his chariots. Deborah and Barak decided to attack him at the point where he was strongest. This meant they would have to attack his nine hundred chariots and troops in the flat Esdraelon Plain. Of course, Sisera was waiting for them.

Deborah did not go with Barak into the actual battle. Since she was a woman, she did not wish to actually lead the troops into battle. She did, however, remind Barak that the Lord would go out before him and would deliver Sisera into Barak's hand (Judges 4:14).

The Great Battle

The location of the battle was near the Kishon River. By not waiting for Sisera to come to him, Barak achieved an element of surprise. But his surprise attack was not enough to give him the victory. The main reason for Israel's triumph was because of what God did.

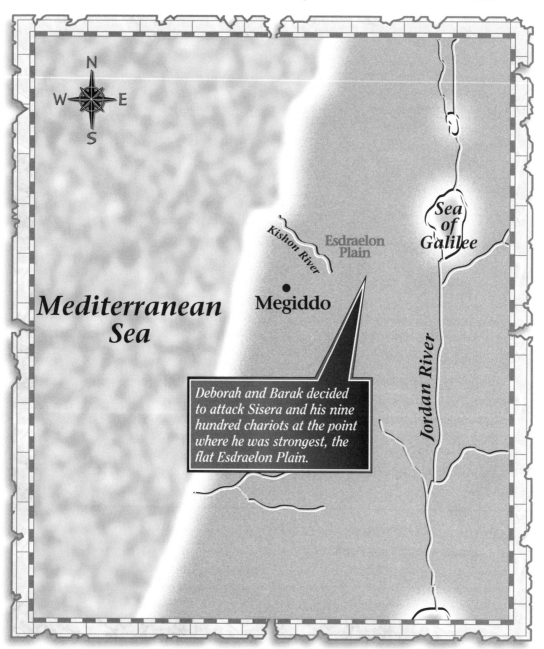

Deborah and Barak decided to attack Sisera and his nine hundred chariots at the point where he was strongest, the flat Esdraelon Plain.

God caused a great rainstorm to develop over the Esdraelon Plain that caused the Kishon River and all its tributaries to overflow their banks. The flooding made Sisera's chariots suddenly more of a hindrance than a help. The chariots became useless as they sank in the mud. The enemy troops were so confused and overwhelmed by what happened that they began to run for their lives. Barak's troops pursued the fleeing Canaanites all the way to their home base in Harosheth Hagoyim. Barak's army succeeded in slaying the fleeing men until "not a man was left" (Judges 4:16).

The Escape and Death of Sisera

But what happened to the great military leader Sisera? Obviously, Sisera saw that the battle was going against him. He knew that he would be defeated if he tried to hold his position. Thus he fled northward in an attempt to reach safety in Hazor. Sisera had trusted in his chariots, but his chariots had totally failed him.

On his way to Hazor, Sisera took refuge in the tent of Heber and Jael. Heber might be described as a "middle-of-the-roader." He did not want to offend either the Canaanites or the Israelites. He wanted to remain at peace with both sides. According to Judges 4:18, it does not sound as if Heber was at home when Sisera arrived. It was Jael, Heber's wife, who came out to meet Sisera.

Jael invited Sisera in and did all she could to make him feel welcome. She gave him both water and milk to drink. She provided a mantle for him to wear and encouraged him to lie down and rest. She even stood watch at the door while he slept.

However, Sisera's sleep quickly turned into a sleep of death. Jael used this opportunity to bring an end to the Canaanite oppression. The nail she took was a tent peg. With crushing blows, she beat and pierced Sisera's skull, fastening the tent peg into the ground.

The Victory Is Complete!

Shortly after Jael killed Sisera, Barak arrived with his troops. He witnessed the fulfillment of what Deborah had earlier predicted—that a woman would receive the honor of slaying his enemy.

Certainly, Barak must have been disappointed that he was not the one who killed Sisera. But he also had the satisfaction of knowing that God used him to bring about the defeat of the Canaanite enemy. The result was complete victory and the end of the Canaanite oppression. Judges 4:24 indicates that Jabin himself, the strong king of Hazor, was later killed. Evidently, Barak followed up the victory by even going against King Jabin in his own city. Since Jabin no longer had a strong army, he was easily defeated and slain.

LESSONS ON LEADERSHIP!

SPIRITUAL COMMITMENT

Deborah's Lesson on Leadership!

To one degree or another, all of the judges demonstrated spiritual commitment. However, Deborah's depth of commitment was remarkable, certainly contributing to her ability to lead her people.

> *"Deborah's depth of commitment was remarkable, certainly contributing to her ability to lead her people."*

First of all, God had honored her as a prophetess. This was an honor that God did not bestow lightly. Second, she approached Barak stating, "Has not the Lord God of Israel commanded . . . ?" (Judges 4:6). She did not try to use her position to make him do something. Rather, she pointed out what God said should be done.

Both Deborah and Barak demonstrated great spiritual commitment by their willingness to trust God and attack Sisera in the Esdraelon Plain. Sisera already had a great troop advantage. Attacking him in the Esdraelon Plain seemed, humanly speaking, like he would have even a greater military advantage.

SONG OF DEBORAH AND BARAK
Judges 5:1–31

Then Deborah and Barak the son of Abinoam sang on that
day, saying:

> When leaders lead in Israel,
> When the people willingly offer themselves,
> Bless the Lord!
>
> Hear, O kings! Give ear, O princes!
> I, even I, will sing to the Lord;
> I will sing praise to the Lord God of Israel.
>
> Lord, when You went out from Seir,
> When You marched from the field of Edom,
> The earth trembled and the heavens poured,
> The clouds also poured water;
> The mountains gushed before the Lord,
> This Sinai, before the Lord God of Israel.
>
> In the days of Shamgar, son of Anath,
> In the days of Jael,
> The highways were deserted,
> And the travelers walked along the byways.
> Village life ceased, it ceased in Israel,
> Until I, Deborah, arose,
> Arose a mother in Israel.
> They chose new gods;
> Then there was war in the gates;
> Not a shield or spear was seen among forty thousand
>   in Israel.
> My heart is with the rulers of Israel
> Who offered themselves willingly with the people.
> Bless the Lord!
>
> Speak, you who ride on white donkeys,
> Who sit in judges' attire,
> And who walk along the road.
> Far from the noise of the archers, among the watering
>   places,

There they shall recount the righteous acts of the
    Lord,
The righteous acts for His villagers in Israel;
Then the people of the Lord shall go down to the gates.

Awake, awake, Deborah!
Awake, awake, sing a song!
Arise, Barak, and lead your captives away,
O son of Abinoam!

Then the survivors came down, the people against the
    nobles;
The Lord came down for me against the mighty.
From Ephraim were those whose roots were in
    Amalek.
After you, Benjamin, with your peoples,
From Machir rulers came down,
And from Zebulun those who bear the recruiter's staff.
And the princes of Issachar were with Deborah;
As Issachar, so was Barak
Sent into the valley under his command;
Among the divisions of Reuben
There were great resolves of heart.
Why did you sit among the sheepfolds,
To hear the pipings for the flocks?
The divisions of Reuben have great searchings of heart.
Gilead stayed beyond the Jordan,
And why did Dan remain on ships?
Asher continued at the seashore,
And stayed by his inlets.
Zebulun is a people who jeopardized their lives to the
    point of death,
Naphtali also, on the heights of the battlefield.

The kings came and fought,
Then the kings of Canaan fought
In Taanach, by the waters of Megiddo;
They took no spoils of silver.
They fought from the heavens;
The stars from their courses fought against Sisera.
The torrent of Kishon swept them away,

That ancient torrent, the torrent of Kishon.
O my soul, march on in strength!
Then the horses' hooves pounded,
The galloping, galloping of his steeds.
"Curse Meroz," said the angel of the Lord,
"Curse its inhabitants bitterly,
Because they did not come to the help of the Lord,
To the help of the Lord against the mighty."

Most blessed among women is Jael,
The wife of Heber the Kenite;
Blessed is she among women in tents.
He asked for water, she gave milk;
She brought out cream in a lordly bowl.
She stretched her hand to the tent peg,
Her right hand to the workmen's hammer;
She pounded Sisera, she pierced his head,
She split and struck through his temple.
At her feet he sank, he fell, he lay still;
At her feet he sank, he fell;
Where he sank, there he fell dead.

The mother of Sisera looked through the window,
And cried out through the lattice,
"Why is his chariot so long in coming?
Why tarries the clatter of his chariots?"
Her wisest ladies answered her,
Yes, she answered herself,
"Are they not finding and dividing the spoil:
To every man a girl or two;
For Sisera, plunder of dyed garments,
Plunder of garments embroidered and dyed,
Two pieces of dyed embroidery for the neck of the
    looter?"

Thus let all Your enemies perish, O Lord!
But let those who love Him be like the sun
When it comes out in full strength.

So the land had rest for forty years.

Then, in writing her song, Deborah further showed her personal commitment to God in the way she gave all the praise to God for the victory. She did not take any of the glory for either herself or Barak. In Judges 5:3, for instance, she wrote, "I, even I, will sing praise to the Lord"; in 5:13, "The Lord came down for me against the mighty." Deborah centered her thoughts upon God and sought to exalt Him in her life and work.

Her spiritual commitment is an important lesson for every Christian, especially those who want to be leaders. When we are totally committed to doing God's will, we know that He will give the victory!

INCREASE YOUR UNDERSTANDING

1. Select three other women in the Bible who were mightily used by God. Describe how God used them to accomplish His purposes.

2. Research the city-state form of government. Identify the weaknesses and strengths of this form of government.

3. Gather information on how iron is produced today. How is this production process different from that used by the Canaanites?

4. Locate other Biblical examples of how God used nature to gain the victory over an enemy.

5. Write a brief paper on the following topic: "The Biblical Responsibilities of Men and Women in the Home, Church, and Community."

PREPARING FOR LEADERSHIP!

1. Sisera trusted in his chariots to deliver him. Both Christians and non-Christians alike trust in many different things to bring them peace, happiness, or even salvation.

   (a) What are some of the things Christians trust to bring them peace, happiness, or success?

   (b) Make a list of those areas in which you are not trusting the Lord completely.

(c) What steps can you take that will help you to trust the Lord more in the areas you have identified?

2. In addition to her spiritual commitment, how else did Deborah demonstrate her leadership ability?

3. Of the four *Lessons on Leadership!* presented so far in your text, which one do you find as the most difficult to achieve in your own life? Why? Which one would be the easiest for you to achieve? Why?

CHAPTER SEVEN

Gideon
The Call
(Judges 6:11–40)

The life of Gideon, a favorite topic in Sunday school, provides a number of valuable lessons for Christians. For this reason, the next two chapters will be devoted to the study of this well-known judge. This week's chapter will emphasize his character and his call by God to deliver Israel from its enemy. The next chapter will focus on the actual battle and deliverance.

As we begin reading in Judges 6, we see Israel is once again in trouble because of its sins. It's the same old story that you have been reading about each time a new judge has been introduced. As Israel disobeys God and falls deeper into sin, God judges the nation by placing it under the bondage of one of the surrounding nations. Eventually, the oppression is more than the people can bear and they cry out to God for deliverance. God, in His mercy, raises up a deliverer (judge) who defeats the enemy nation and restores Israel's freedom. Although the people vow to serve and obey God, it is only a short time before the cycle of sin and deliverance begins once again.

Israel's Cycle of Sin and Deliverance

- The Nation Served God
- The Nation Did Evil
- The Nation Forsook God
- The Nation Followed Its Own Way (Pleasure)
- The Nation Was Sold into Slavery (Depression and War)
- The Nation in Slavery
- The Nation in Servitude
- The Nation Cried Out to God
- The Nation Turned to God
- The Nation Repented
- God Raised Up Judges
- The Nation Was Delivered

A New Generation of Israelites

Again and again the Israelites went their own way and returned to sinning. Why did this continue to happen? The answer is really quite simple. The Israelites who had experienced the oppression of the Canaanites during the time of Deborah and Barak were no longer living. A new generation of Israelites were now living in the land. They obviously had not learned the lessons from their ancestors for they were committing the same sins that had caused the previous oppressions.

"And the children of Israel did evil in the sight of the Lord. So the Lord delivered them into the hand of Midian for seven years" (Judges 6:1).

In Judges 6:1 we see that Israel was in trouble again. This time God used the Midianites to punish the people. The Midianites employed unusual battle tactics. Some would call it a hit-and-run technique. The Midianites would keep to themselves during certain times of the year. After the Israelites had prepared their ground, planted their crops, tended to them, and were ready to harvest them, the Midianites would come in and steal all of the crops. This was an effective system for the Midianites, but the Israelites were about to starve!

God used these tactics of the Midianites to bring Israel to the place of repentance. It was almost as if God was telling the Israelites that they needed spiritual food more than physical food. God had always taken care of their physical need for food. Hadn't He provided manna and quail while the nation wandered for forty years in the wilderness? Now Israel was concerned about physical food again. Yet it was spiritual food that they really needed. Their hearts had grown cold toward God, and they had turned from doing His will.

Gideon Is Chosen

The next judge was Gideon, a young man. Gideon lived in Ophrah, a village of Manasseh, likely located in the Esdraelon Valley where the Midianite attacks had been centered. The Midianites were probably nearby because Judges 6:11 says that Gideon was threshing wheat in a winepress in order to hide it from the Midianites.

The angel of the Lord appeared to Gideon while he was busy threshing the wheat. The angel addressed Gideon as "you mighty

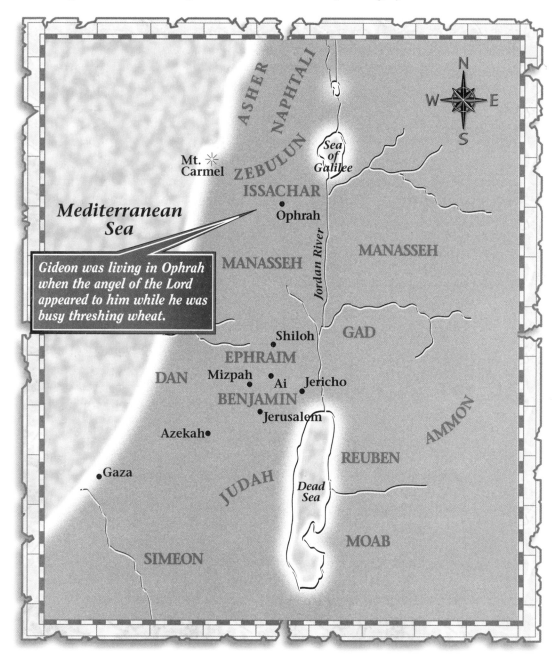

Gideon was living in Ophrah when the angel of the Lord appeared to him while he was busy threshing wheat.

man of valor." It is quite certain that Gideon did not see himself as a mighty man of valor. However, God saw Gideon as what he could be—in His strength—not as what he was in his own weakness. God knew that Gideon would prove to be a mighty warrior.

Before Gideon received instructions, he received assurance from the angel that God would help him. At first, Gideon expressed doubt that God would actually deliver the Israelites from their enemy. In Gideon's eyes, the Midianites were too strong to be defeated. Besides, the Midianites had been taking Israel's crops for seven years! Gideon told the angel that it seemed like God really had forsaken His people.

It is interesting to note that the angel did not rebuke Gideon for his apparent unbelief. Rather, the angel insisted that Gideon show courage and faithfully do as God had spoken.

Gideon was instructed to bring unleavened bread and a young goat as an offering to the Lord. He did as he was told. When he returned, he placed the offering on a rock. The angel of the Lord stretched forth His staff, and the entire offering was consumed by fire. The angel of the Lord then departed from Gideon. It was at that moment that Gideon realized that he had truly been in the Lord's presence. Now Gideon was ready for the task God was to set before him.

Gideon's Personal Preparation Begins

God's first assignment for Gideon was not to directly attack the enemy, as might be expected. Gideon's first assignment was to destroy the offensive evidence of Baal worship in the community. The Baal "high places" were the center of the pagan worship. Interestingly, one of the most important of the Baal high places was located on the property of Gideon's father, Joash.

BIBLE BACKGROUND

Baal Worship

Baal, which means "lord" or "master," could be used as a title for any person who owned something, or any god considered to be a lord or master. The word *Baal* soon became identified with various regional gods that were thought to provide fertility for crops and livestock. As a god who symbolized the productive forces of nature, Baal worship often included various forms of sensuality.

Baal appears in the Bible in many forms and under many different names. The Bible frequently makes reference to the Baals (the plural of Baal). The word *Baal* was often used in the forming of names, such as Baal-Berith, which means "lord of the covenant." This is just one of the names under which Baal was worshiped during the time of the judges.

PAGAN GODS MENTIONED IN THE BIBLE

Name in NKJV	Description	Biblical Reference
Adrammelech	A Babylonian god worshiped by the Sepharvites	2 Kings 17:31
Anammelech	A Babylonian god worshiped by the Sepharvites	2 Kings 17:31
Asherah	The wife of Baal in Canaanite mythology	1 Kings 18:19
Ashima	A Hittite god worshiped by the people of Hamath	2 Kings 17:30
Ashtoreth	The Syrian and Phoenician goddess of the moon, sexual love, and fertility	2 Kings 23:13
Ashtoreths	The plural form of Ashtoreth	Judges 10:6
Baal	The chief male deity of the Phoenicians and Canaanites	Numbers 22:41
Baal-Berith	A name under which Baal was worshiped in the time of the judges	Judges 9:4
Baal of Peor	An idol of Moab, probably the same as Chemosh	Psalms 106:28
Baals	The plural form of Baal	Judges 8:33
Baal-Zebub	A name under which Baal was worshiped at the Philistine city of Ekron	2 Kings 1:2–3
Beelzebub	A heathen god considered by the Jews to be the supreme evil spirit	Mark 3:22
Bel	A god identified with Marduk, chief Babylonian god	Isaiah 46:1
Chemosh	The national god of the Moabites and Ammonites	Jeremiah 48:7, 13
Chiun	A star-god, identified with Saturn	Amos 5:26
Dagon	The chief god of the Philistines	1 Samuel 5:2–7
Diana	In Roman mythology, the goddess of the moon hunting, wild animals, and virginity	Acts 19:24, 27–28
Gad	A pagan god worshiped by the Israelites along with Meni	Isaiah 65:11
Gold calf	An idol made by the Israelites in the wilderness	Exodus 32
Hermes	The Greek god of commerce, science, invention, cunning, eloquence, and theft	Acts 14:12
Mammon	The Aramaic word for riches, personified by Jesus as a false god	Luke 16:9, 11
Meni	A heathen deity worshiped by the Israelites along with Gad	Isaiah 65:11
Merodach	The Babylonian god of war and the patron deity of the city of Babylon	Jeremiah 50:2
Milcom	Another name for Molech	1 Kings 11:5
Molech	National god of the Ammonites whose worship involved child sacrifice	Leviticus 18:21
Moloch	Another name for Molech	Acts 7:43
Nebo	The Babylonian god of literature, wisdom, and the arts	Isaiah 46:1
Nehushtan	The name given to Moses' bronze serpent when people began to worship it	2 Kings 18:4
Nergal	The war god of the men of Cuth, in Media-Persia	2 Kings 17:30
Nibhaz	An idol worshiped by the Avites	2 Kings 17:31
Nisroch	An Assyrian god with a temple in Nineveh	Isaiah 37:38
Remphan	An idol worshiped by Israel in the wilderness, perhaps the same as Chiun	Acts 7:43
Rimmon	The Assyrian god of rain, lightning, and thunder	2 Kings 5:18
Sikkuth	A name given by the Babylonians to the planet Saturn	Amos 5:26
Succoth Benoth	A Babylonian goddess, the mistress of Marduk	2 Kings 17:30
Tammuz	A Babylonian fertility god	Ezekiel 8:14
Tartak	An idol worshiped by the Avites	2 Kings 17:31
Twin Brothers	In Greek mythology, the twin sons of Zeus	Acts 28:11
Zeus	The supreme god of the ancient Greeks	Acts 14:12–13

This was a very difficult assignment for Gideon. However, it was a necessary lesson in faith and courage that would prepare him for the battle ahead. Gideon used ten of his personal servants—possibly because he couldn't rely on anyone else—and did the work at night (Judges 6:27).

Gideon and his ten men must have worked at a feverish pace to do so much in the few hours of darkness. They destroyed the Baal altar, cut down an Asherah pole (a pole set up next to the Baal altar, signifying worship through sexual acts) and prepared it for fuel, built a new altar to the true God, and prepared a bullock to sacrifice on it.

> "And Joash said to all who stood against him, 'Would you plead for Baal? Would you save him? Let the one who would plead for him be put to death by morning! If he is a god, let him plead for himself, because his altar has been torn down!'"
> (Judges 6:31).

The next morning, when the people of the village learned what had happened, they were enraged. They went to Joash, demanding that Gideon be put to death. At this point, Joash demonstrated that he was a very wise man. He told the people that if Baal was god, he was certainly capable of punishing Gideon himself. Rather than the people taking out their vengeance on Gideon, they should let Baal do it.

The people were astonished at Joash's words, yet did as he advised. Gideon was left alone, all night, near Baal. When morning came and Gideon was unharmed, he was given an additional name, "Jerubbaal," meaning "Let Baal contend." This name indicated a new reputation for Gideon in the community because he had successfully stood up to Baal and had not been harmed.

In spite of this obvious victory over Baal, Gideon was still uneasy about the call of God to lead a battle against the Midianites. He still was not sure whether or not God really had selected him to deliver Israel.

It would be easy to criticize Gideon for his continued lack of faith. But how many of us would have moved forward into battle facing the odds that Gideon faced? Gideon had raised an army of thirty-two thousand troops. However, he described the Midianites as "numerous as locusts" (Judges 6:5). Later we actually learn that the Midianite army consisted of 135,000 troops (Judges 8:10)—over four times larger than Gideon's! Gideon certainly had good reason to be afraid.

Gideon once again sought assurance from God by what has become well known as his test with "a fleece of wool" (Judges 6:36–40). Gideon placed the fleece on the ground and asked God to make it wet that night, while leaving the ground dry. He stated that if God would be pleased to do this, he, Gideon, would then know that God would truly "save Israel" by his hand. God graciously did as Gideon requested. The next morning, Gideon was able to wring a bowl of water from the fleece.

Even though God performed this miracle, Gideon was still not sure that God would give him the victory. Thus he asked God to perform another miracle the following night, this time by making all the ground wet and leaving the fleece dry. The next morning Gideon found that God had once again done as he had asked. Finally, Gideon was convinced of God's blessing upon his leadership.

> "Gideon placed the fleece on the ground and asked God to make it wet that night, while leaving the ground dry. He stated that if God would be pleased to do this, he, Gideon would then know that God would truly 'save Israel' by his hand."

God certainly knew Gideon's heart. He knew that Gideon would be a faithful and obedient leader. However, God also knew that Gideon needed assurance that he would be victorious. These practical illustrations of God's power prepared Gideon for the upcoming battle.

Now that Gideon was assured of God's blessing, it was time to go to work. There was so much to do. An army had to be assembled and trained. A battle strategy had to be developed. The nation of Israel would need to rally around his leadership. Regardless of the many challenges facing him, Gideon knew that God had chosen him to deliver Israel from the hands of the Midianites.

MAINTAINING A GODLY TESTIMONY AT HOME

Gideon's Lesson on Leadership!

Maintaining a Godly Testimony at Home may seem like an unusual leadership lesson. But the story of Gideon's preparation for his battle with the Midianites began right in his hometown. In order for Gideon's men to follow his leadership into battle, they needed to know that he was a man of character that could be trusted. If Gideon was going to trust God to provide victory over the Midianites, then Gideon had to first trust God to give him victory over the false god, Baal. For it was Baal who was being worshiped right in Gideon's own home.

Many times it is more difficult to share your testimony and live righteously among your friends and family than it is among total strangers. One of the true tests of your character and ability to lead is demonstrated by the way you conduct your life around those who know you best. Gideon passed the test, will you?

INCREASE YOUR UNDERSTANDING

1. The angel of the Lord appears at very strategic times in Israel's history. Research the appearances of the angel of the Lord as well as the differing opinions regarding the identification of this angel.

2. There are a number of pagan gods identified in the Bible. From the list provided in this chapter, choose a god or goddess that has also been mentioned in your history or English class. How does your history or reading textbook portray the pagan god or goddess mentioned in the Bible?

3. Gideon had to demonstrate great faith if he was to go into battle against a Midianite army consisting of at least 135,000 troops. Give three examples of other individuals in the Bible who had to demonstrate great faith to carry out God's plan.

4. Identify the New Testament references to Baal worship. What additional information do you learn about Baal worship that helps you better understand Gideon's situation?

5. Conduct further research on the Midianites. Be sure that you address the following questions:

(a) What do other Biblical passages tell us about the Midianites?

(b) Who were their ancestors?

(c) Had they posed problems for Israel before?

(d) How would you describe the way they lived? What did they believe?

PREPARING FOR LEADERSHIP!

Suppose your friend, Jim, came to you and said the following, "I can share my faith with others, but I can't seem to talk to my dad about his need to know Jesus Christ as his personal Savior." How would you respond? Prepare a one-page response to your friend's question. Be sure that your response provides specific examples of what Jim could say to his father. Once you have completed your one-page response, ask one of your parents to review what you have written. Note his or her comments and be prepared to share the comments in class.

CHAPTER EIGHT

Gideon

Strange Way to Win a War

(Judges 7:1–8:23)

Now that Gideon had successfully completed God's training program, it was time to prepare for the actual battle. Gideon's character had been put to the test. He was now ready to prepare for war. Gideon had to gather his troops, train them, and then develop a battle plan.

But Gideon was soon to learn another important lesson from God. This time there would be no doubt that God was in control and that He would provide complete victory over the Midianites.

Preparation for Battle

Gideon knew he faced a difficult battle; so he did his best to make all the proper preparations. He especially wanted to make sure that he had enough good fighting men. He enlisted the help of thirty-two thousand Israelite soldiers.

But as Gideon looked out over his army, he was convinced that he did not have enough men to successfully defeat the enemy. The Midianites were like grasshoppers on the hills. They easily outnumbered the Israelites.

Before Gideon had the chance to call for more troops, God made an unusual demand of him. God told Gideon that he had *too many* soldiers and that he would have to get rid of some. God was interested in demonstrating to the Israelites that He would deliver them from the Midianites. If thirty-two thousand men had won the battle, Israel could boast that they had overpowered the Midianites by their own strength. God had to teach the people of Israel that He alone gave the victory.

God instructed Gideon to reduce the size of his army by letting every soldier who was "fearful and afraid" go home. This was certainly not what Gideon wanted to hear, but he obeyed God. Gideon must have been shocked when twenty-two thousand of his men departed. Possibly Gideon was hoping that only a few hundred would leave. But now he was left with only ten thousand men to fight tens of thousands of Midianites.

> *"And the Lord said to Gideon, 'The people who are with you are too many for Me to give the Midianites into their hands, lest Israel claim glory for itself against Me, saying, "My own hand has saved me" ' "* (Judges 7:2).

God, however, was not yet through with the matter of reducing the size of Gideon's army. The army was still too large if credit was to be given to God for the coming victory. God then came to Gideon with new instructions.

Gideon was now told to reduce the size of his army by means of a test at a nearby stream. Gideon was to bring his remaining ten thousand men there and observe how each drank the water. Those who drank by bringing water up to their mouths by hand were to be kept in the army (Judges 7:6). Those who "got down on their knees to drink water" were to be sent home.

The reason for this test was obvious. Those troops who brought the water up to their mouths by hand demonstrated their readiness to meet the enemy by being in a position to see the enemy approaching. Those who bowed their heads to drink were obviously more interested in their personal needs than in being ready to fight. This meant that the first group would make better soldiers than the second.

Gideon did as God instructed. According to the Bible 9,700 of his soldiers bowed their heads and lapped water from the stream like a dog. Only three hundred of his soldiers demonstrated their readiness for battle by bringing the water up to their mouths by hand. How could Gideon ever hope to defeat the Midianites with only three hundred men?

God's Encouragement to Gideon

With such a small army available to him, Gideon must have been both worried and depressed. But God was aware of Gideon's discouragement and comforted him by providing a clear sign that Gideon would be victorious. God always demonstrates His love and concern for His children.

God's encouragement to Gideon came in two ways: a direct statement and a field trip. In Judges 7:7, God tells Gideon that in spite of how impossible the situation looked, He would give the victory to Gideon and his army of three hundred. Gideon did not have to be afraid. God was in control of the situation. Certainly, it must have been an encouragement to Gideon to hear these words from the Lord.

However, God also wanted to give Gideon additional proof that the Midianites would be defeated. So he sent Gideon on a field trip. God told Gideon to walk down to the camp of the Midianites the following night so that he might hear what would be said there. Gideon took one of his servants, Purah, and went down to the Midianite camp.

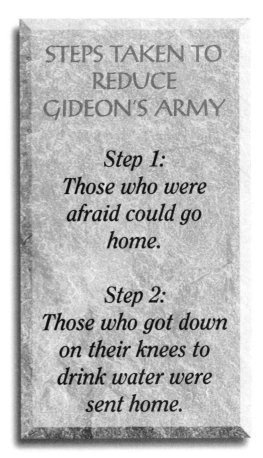

STEPS TAKEN TO REDUCE GIDEON'S ARMY

Step 1:
Those who were afraid could go home.

Step 2:
Those who got down on their knees to drink water were sent home.

Coming near to one of the tents of the enemy, Gideon overheard one Midianite tell another of a dream he just had. The man said that "a loaf of barley bread" tumbled into the camp of Midian, then struck a Midianite tent and made it fall. Gideon heard the other man respond that this loaf of barley bread signified the coming of Gideon. The flattened Midianite tent showed that Gideon would be victorious when he came.

After overhearing the conversation, Gideon and Purah returned to their camp. What they heard must have also been a great encouragement to them. They were now confident that God would give Israel victory over the Midianites.

Gideon and His Army Go to Battle

There is probably no battle in the Old Testament that is better known than this one. As the battle opens, the enemy is encamped in the Esdraelon Valley at a point between Mount Gilboa on the south and Mount Moreh on the north. Gideon's men were grouped near the well of Harod at the foot of Mount Gilboa.

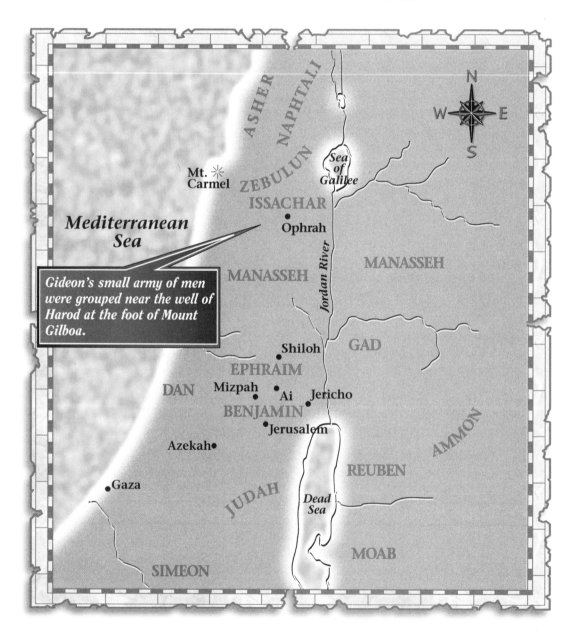

Gideon's small army of men were grouped near the well of Harod at the foot of Mount Gilboa.

Not only was Gideon going to war with a small army, but he was also using some very strange weapons. The weapons consisted of lamps, pitchers, and trumpets. The lamps were hidden inside the pitchers, which—being made of pottery—could be broken easily.

Gideon's army moved out at midnight, just after the setting of the middle watch. The middle watch of a night often was the best time to attack because the sentries would be more sleepy and less alert than at other times of the night. Gideon's army would have a much better chance for a surprise attack.

Gideon had divided his men into three companies, one hundred in each company. Each company was sent to a separate location. They probably all stayed on the mountainside, however, where their lamps could be easily seen by the enemy below.

When everything was ready, Gideon gave the sign. All three companies blew their trumpets and broke their pitchers. Immediately, the Midianites heard a great noise from the blowing of the trumpets and the breaking of the pitchers and saw a burst of bright light from the three hundred lamps. The enemy was taken by complete surprise and fled in panic, thinking that a great army had come upon them. They headed for the Jordan River and shortest route home.

Gideon was not content to just let the Midianites escape. He was determined to thoroughly defeat them. Thus he quickly sent word to the Ephraimites to cut off the enemy's escape at the Jordan. The Ephraimites responded and killed two Midianite leaders, Oreb and Zeeb.

Gideon's troops were joined by men from the tribes of Naphtali, Asher, and Manasseh (Judges 7:23). Many of these men were undoubtedly those who left or were sent away from Gideon's army

> *"Gideon's troops were joined by men from the tribes of Naphtali, Asher, and Manasseh (Judges 7:23)."*

during the time of the troop reduction. But now they returned to assist Gideon and his forces against their common enemy.

The battle was a total victory for Gideon and his men. Although his army was small and his weapons unusual, God gave him the victory. Upon his return home, Gideon was praised as a mighty warrior and deliverer. The people were so grateful that the Midianite oppression was over that they wanted to make Gideon king. However, he refused because he knew that God alone was to receive the praise and glory for his victory over the Midianites.

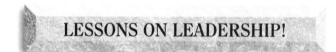

LESSONS ON LEADERSHIP!

LARGE NUMBERS ARE NOT NEEDED FOR GREAT RESULTS

Gideon's Second Lesson on Leadership!

It is often assumed that the importance or effectiveness of a leader is determined by the number of people he or she commands. But the story of Gideon certainly demonstrates that this is not true. The victory over the Midianites illustrated that God is not dependent on large numbers of human participants to win the battle. This battle also illustrates that the quality of Gideon's soldiers was far more important than the quantity. Gideon's army of three hundred was small, but it was composed of dedicated individuals.

Large Numbers Are Not Needed for Great Results is an important and practical *Lesson on Leadership!* As Gideon finally learned, the success of his leadership was dependent upon God. Gideon's success was not in numbers. His success was the result of obeying God, no matter what God asked him to do.

1. Through the dream of a Midianite, God assured Gideon that he would be victorious. There are many examples in the Bible of God using dreams to reveal His plans. Why do you think God used dreams in this way? In your opinion, what are the three most interesting dreams in the Old Testament that God used? Explain why you selected these three.

2. Research Oreb and Zeeb, the Midianite leaders.

3. Gideon gave the Ephraimites the responsibility of cutting off the Midianite escape at the Jordan River. Why was this responsibility given to the tribe of Ephraim?

PREPARING FOR LEADERSHIP!

Anyone who has ever served in a position of leadership knows that there are times in which you are afraid. Strong leaders do not flee in the face of fear. Effective, godly leaders realize that God is in total control of every situation. The following questions will help you gain a better understanding of how leaders respond to fear.

1. Give three examples of great military leaders that must have experienced times of fear. How do you think they overcame their fears?

2. Who do you think is the greatest leader living today? What types of fears do you think this person experiences? How do you think he or she overcomes these fears?

3. After reviewing this week's chapter, list the times that Gideon experienced fear. How did God encourage him during each of these times?

CHAPTER NINE

Abimelech
The Renegade King
(Judges 9)

It is now time to take a break in the action as we consider Abimelech, the renegade king. The story of Abimelech is unique in the book of Judges. Abimelech was not a judge and he did not deliver the country from any outside oppressor. Rather he was crowned as a king in Shechem, ruled wickedly for three years, and then died a humiliating death as punishment from God.

Since the story of Abimelech is different from any other story in the book of Judges, some have wondered why it was even included. However, as you will soon see, the story of Abimelech has a number of important spiritual lessons.

Abimelech's Plot

If you were ever looking for an Old Testament crime story, this would be it. Judges 9 is full of murder, bloodshed, and conspiracy. It all focuses on one man: Abimelech, the son of Gideon.

Peace was once again broken after Gideon's death. But this time it was broken by Gideon's son Abimelech and not an enemy nation. Abimelech's actions brought three years of war and treachery to Israel.

Abimelech was neither a peace-loving nor humble man. What he wanted was the throne. Although Gideon refused a kingship, Abimelech would do anything to obtain it.

> *"Then he went to his father's house at Ophrah and killed his brothers, the seventy sons of Jerubbaal, on one stone. But Jotham the youngest son of Jerubbaal was left, because he hid himself"* (Judges 9:5).

After the death of his father, he came to Shechem to persuade the elders of the city to make him king.

Abimelech must have had a persuasive personality because those who heard him were convinced by his words. They were so convinced that he should be king that they went to the other leaders of the city to tell them about this wonderful and talented young man.

In the meantime, Abimelech obtained money from the Baal temple and used it to hire men who would help him get what he wanted. These men used threats and violence to assist Abimelech to convince the people that he should be king. Soon after Abimelech hired his outlaw helpers, he traveled north to the city of Ophrah to commit one of the most terrible murders recorded in the Old Testament.

BIBLE BACKGROUND

What Is a Parable?

A parable is a short, simple story designed to communicate a spiritual truth; a religious principle or a moral lesson. A parable is a figure of speech in which truth is illustrated by a comparison or example drawn from everyday experiences.

Even though Jesus was a master at using parables, He was not the first to use them. Although parables are most frequently found in the New Testament, examples of parables are found throughout the Old Testament.

In order to ensure that he alone would become king, he had his seventy brothers slaughtered. Only the youngest brother, Jotham, was able to escape. Once the murders were completed, Abimelech returned to Shechem and arranged for his actual coronation. Since the people believed that all of his brothers were dead, Abimelech was crowned king.

Jotham's Parable

Jotham, Gideon's youngest son, survived the slaughter. Somehow he was able to escape from Abimelech's men and save his own life. He quickly went to Mount Gerizim to address the people of Shechem. He knew he wouldn't have much time to speak, for Abimelech would soon find him and seek to destroy him. From his place on Mount Gerizim, he shouted forth a parable to the Shechemites clearly illustrating what was taking place.

Jotham's parable concerned the selection by a group of trees of one of their own number to rule them. The kingship was first offered to the olive tree, but this tree refused by asking why it should cease giving its oil, for which people give honor to both God and man, simply to be promoted to "sway over the trees."

The position was then offered to the fig tree, but this tree refused by asking why it should leave its "sweetness" and "good fruit" to be promoted. Third, the kingship was offered to the vine, but the vine further refused by asking why it should leave its "wine," which cheers both God and man, for this promotion. Each of these important fruit producers refused the kingship offered to it on the basis that it had more important functions to perform.

Finally, the position was offered to the lowly bramble. To the surprise of everyone, this useless plant accepted. Not only did it accept, but it did so by saying, "Come and take shelter in my shade; but if not, let fire come out of the bramble and devour the cedars of Lebanon!" (Judges 9:15).

> *Olive tree refused because . . . it provided food and nourishment.*
>
> *Fig tree refused because . . . it provided sweetness and enjoyment.*
>
> *Vine refused because . . . it provided cheer and happiness.*

Jotham then explained the meaning of his parable. The Shechemites, by crowning Abimelech as king, had chosen one who was like the bramble, in comparison to the olive tree, the fig tree, and the grapevine. The bramble was worthless, hardly good enough for burning as fuel, while the others all produced fine fruit.

Then Jotham reminded the people of the good work of his father, Gideon. He reminded them of his great victory over the Midianites. But then he told the Shechemites what Abimelech had done. He told them how Abimelech massacred Gideon's sons and that he, Jotham, was the only one who escaped. Finally, Jotham told the people that they dishonored Gideon by making Abimelech king. He pronounced a curse on the city and then fled. He knew that Abimelech would soon come looking for him.

The Shechemites Revolt

Abimelech ruled the city of Shechem for the next three years. However, it was not a peaceful time. Abimelech's evil ways caused great hardship for the people. Finally, they had enough of Abimelech and revolted. Their leader in the revolt was a man named Gaal, the head of a roving band of outlaws.

Gaal was certainly no better than Abimelech. He was a drunkard and a vile man. He boasted that he should be the one to rule Shechem and was determined to kill Abimelech. The Shechemites had already made one mistake by making Abimelech their king. Now they were about to enlist another wicked man to lead them.

Zebul, the local ruler of the city, was angered by Gaal's words. Thus he sent word to Abimelech of what was going on. Zebul told Abimelech how to invade and conquer the city, thus defeating Gaal and his army. Abimelech did as Zebul instructed him, and Gaal was defeated.

The next day Abimelech prepared to attack Shechem. As he approached the city, the people came out to do battle with him. The very people Abimelech thought he could count on were those who had now turned against him. Abimelech and his army easily defeated the people. The Bible records that Abimelech not only killed many of the Shechemites, but that he also destroyed the city and then sowed salt in all the surrounding ground.

By sowing the countryside and the city with salt, the soil could no longer produce. This would remind future generations of what had taken place. Abimelech completed his devastation by burning the tower of Shechem and all those who were hiding inside. The curse recorded at the conclusion of Jotham's parable had been fulfilled. The city of Shechem had been destroyed by the very man that they had chosen to rule over them.

The Death of Abimelech

Abimelech met his death in a very unusual way. After he had destroyed Shechem, he led his army against the neighboring city of Thebez. It was his intent to destroy all of the cities in the surrounding area. He wanted to prove that he was in total control and would not tolerate any rebellion by the people.

The main part of the city of Thebez was easily taken. Many of the people fled for refuge to the city's strong tower. When Abimelech saw where the people were going, he followed the same battle strategy that he had used against the city of Shechem. He used fire to force the people to come out of their stronghold. It would then be very easy for the army to kill them. However, this time something totally unexpected happened.

As Abimelech came close to the tower to personally light the fire, he came within range of a brave woman who was looking down from a window above. As soon as he was close enough, she dropped a millstone upon his head. The millstone she used was probably about ten to fourteen inches long and weighed about five pounds. If dropped upon the head of someone, it could be deadly.

It's possible the stone did not land directly upon Abimelech's head because he was able to talk after being struck. But he obviously knew that he was going to die. Thus he called his armor-bearer to kill him with his sword. Abimelech was a very proud man. He didn't want it said that a woman had killed him. The armor-bearer did as he was instructed. It was a humiliating defeat for Abimelech.

Abimelech's kingship lasted only three years. Upon his death, his followers returned to their homes. It can certainly be said that pride characterized Abimelech's life. The sin of pride caused him to want to be king. This desire to be king led to the death of his brothers and the slaying of many innocent people. This attitude of pride was still evident at his death. As he lay dying, he was more concerned with how people would remember him than how he stood in God's sight.

Pride is a serious sin that can cause people to do terrible things. A prideful individual is totally focused upon himself. He or she is

> *"It can certainly be said that pride characterized Abimelech's life. The sin of pride caused him to want to be king. This desire to be king led to the death of his brothers and the slaying of many innocent people."*

unaware of the feelings or concerns of others. The only thing that matters is personal gain and glory.

Throughout the centuries, history has recorded the wicked deeds of men and women consumed by pride. Whereas man may boast in his accomplishments, God responds that He hates pride and arrogance (Proverbs 8:13).

The next time you are tempted to respond in a prideful way, remember the story of Abimelech and the words of Proverbs 11:2:

> "When pride comes, then comes shame;
> But with the humble is wisdom."

INCREASE YOUR UNDERSTANDING

1. Although Gideon had rejected the kingship, he had still lived a kingly lifestyle. Because Gideon had so many sons, he obviously had many wives. Kings typically had many wives. Research Gideon's life to determine other ways in which Gideon demonstrated a kingly lifestyle. Explain how Gideon's actions may have affected Abimelech.

2. Pride is a serious sin. Using a concordance, describe what the Bible says about pride. Identify a current example of how pride has affected a situation or someone you know.

PREPARING FOR LEADERSHIP!

Becoming a godly leader requires learning positive characteristics from good leaders and identifying the wrong actions of weak or wicked leaders. Abimelech's leadership as an evil king provides us with a number of important lessons.

Note each of the following statements made about King Abimelech. After each statement, cite the verse (or verses) that supports the statement and then the application that you can make to your life as you prepare to assume positions of leadership.

Sin leads to more sin.

Verse(s):

Application:

A lust for power can lead to wicked actions.

Verse(s):

Application:

Evil plans will eventually be discovered.

Verse(s):

Application:

We reap what we sow.

Verse(s):

Application:

CHAPTER TEN

Ruth

Happiness and Hope

(Ruth 1–4)

Although the book of Ruth follows immediately after the book of Judges, her story occurs during the period of the judges. Actually, her story takes place at the time of the five minor judges who will be studied in the next chapter.

The story outlined in the book of Judges has been a gloomy reminder of what happens when a nation disobeys God. However, the story of Ruth is a reminder that life in Israel was not all gloom and doom during this time. Her story presents a happy picture as well as a future hope for the nation of Israel. The study of the book of Judges would not be complete without reviewing the story of Ruth.

Ruth Chooses to Go with Naomi (Ruth 1)

Ruth was a citizen of Moab. She married into an Israelite family that came to her country during a time of famine in Israel. The father of the Israelite family was named Elimelech and the mother's name was Naomi. They had come from Bethlehem.

Elimelech and Naomi had two sons, Mahlon and Chilion. Ruth married Mahlon. Another Moabitess, Orpah, married Chilion. In a matter of just a few years, Elimelech, Mahlon, and Chilion all died. All three women were now widows.

After ten years had passed, it was reported that the famine was over in Judah. Naomi decided that she wanted to return home to Bethlehem. Both daughters-in-law started to go with her, but Naomi tried to talk them out of making the difficult trip. Orpah stayed in Moab, but Ruth told Naomi that she wanted to go with her to Bethlehem. Even though Ruth was not an Israelite, she said, "For wherever you go, I will go; and wherever you lodge, I will lodge;

your people shall be my people, and your God, my God" (Ruth 1:16). So both women departed for Bethlehem.

Ruth Works in the Field of Boaz (Ruth 2)

It was barley harvest time in Judah when Naomi and Ruth arrived in Bethlehem. Ruth volunteered to work in one of the fields to help

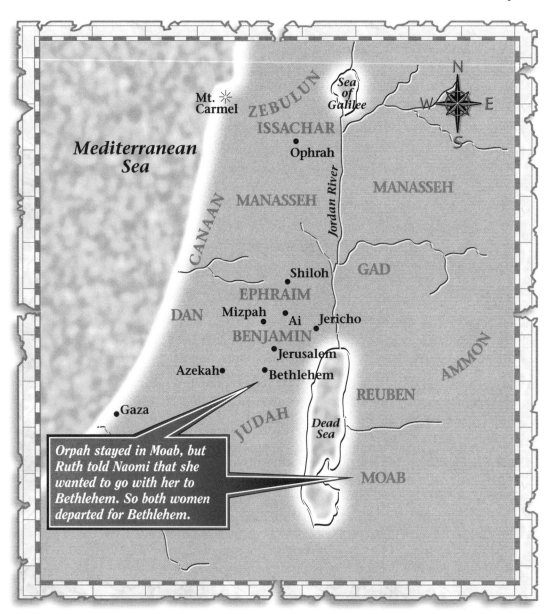

Orpah stayed in Moab, but Ruth told Naomi that she wanted to go with her to Bethlehem. So both women departed for Bethlehem.

support the two of them. The field she happened to work in belonged to a wealthy farmer named Boaz. Although Ruth did not know it, Boaz was a close relative of her deceased father-in-law Elimelech.

When Boaz came to Bethlehem, he noticed the new worker in his field. He was obviously attracted to her. After finding out who she was, he spoke kindly to her. He welcomed her and immediately provided the same wages and provisions that he gave to his other servants.

Ruth was very surprised at his immediate generosity. Boaz told her of his knowledge that she had been very kind to her mother-in-law, Naomi, by making the difficult trip from Moab to Bethlehem. He wanted to show generosity to Ruth for the kindness she had shown to Naomi.

Of course, when Ruth returned home that evening she told Naomi everything that happened that day. Naomi then told Ruth of the relationship of Boaz to Elimelech. They both rejoiced that God had provided so well for their needs.

Ruth Proposes Marriage to Boaz (Ruth 3)

Over time, Ruth and Boaz had the opportunity to become better acquainted. One day, Naomi suggested to Ruth that since Boaz was her "kinsman-redeemer," she should propose marriage to him.

At first this may seem like a strange request, but that is simply because we do not understand the kinsman-redeemer obligation that was practiced during Old Testament times. According to the kinsman-redeemer obligation, the brother of a deceased husband was responsible to marry the brother's widow so that a son might be born to carry on the dead brother's name. This son would then become the heir of the dead brother's property.

Although Boaz was the second-nearest relative, he was the one whom Ruth wanted to fulfill the kinsman-redeemer obligation. If Boaz chose to become her kinsman-redeemer, he would first have to obtain the permission of the nearest relative. Naomi encouraged Ruth to request that Boaz fulfill his obligation to her.

BIBLE BACKGROUND

"kinsman-redeemer"

In the Old Testament, a kinsman is a male relative who shares the same racial, cultural, or national background as another. The word *kinsman* is most often used as a translation of a Hebrew word that means "one who has the right to redeem."

Since an Israelite could sell himself, his family or his land in cases of poverty (Leviticus 25:39–43), the kinsman-redeemer was provided to protect the family (Leviticus 25:25). This person, a near relative, had the first option by law to buy any land being sold, thus allowing it to be kept within the family (Leviticus 25:23–28; Jeremiah 32:6–10).

Frequently, when the husband died, the widow would be unable to support herself and her children. In order to secure enough money to live, she would be forced to sell everything she had. In order to prevent this from happening, the kinsman-redeemer obligation was instituted. A male relative, who was closely related to the deceased husband, could marry the widow. Thus she and her children would be taken care of.

On a spiritual level, God is the kinsman who redeems. In the Old Testament, the focus of God's redemptive activity is the Exodus where He delivered Israel from the slavery of Egypt (Deuteronomy 7:8; 2 Samuel 7:23). In the New Testament, Jesus is described as our brother (Hebrews 2:11), who redeems us from the power of sin.

Since Ruth knew where Boaz slept, one night she went in to sleep at the foot of his bed. When he awoke the next morning, he asked her why she was there. She identified herself and asked him to take her "under his wing." This act signified a husband and wife relationship.

In other words, she made her proposal of marriage to him. She reminded him of his kinsman responsibility.

Boaz told Ruth that he would accept her proposal. Not only did he desire to fulfill his kinsman-redeemer obligation, but the Biblical story also implies that he had fallen in love with Ruth.

Upon returning home, Naomi wanted to know what happened. She wanted to know if Boaz accepted Ruth's proposal. Then Ruth showed Naomi the six measures of barley that Boaz gave her. It was clear that Boaz loved her and intended to marry her.

Boaz Marries Ruth (Ruth 4)

On the following morning, Boaz took steps to carry out his promise to marry Ruth. Boaz went to the city gate to find Ruth's closest relative to see if he wanted to fulfill the kinsman-redeemer obligation.

The man replied that he would be Ruth's kinsman-redeemer. He was obviously interested in her property that he would inherit.

But then Boaz informed him that as kinsman-redeemer, he would also need to marry Ruth. Upon hearing this, the man indicated that he could not serve as her kinsman-redeemer. Although the reason is not fully known, Ruth's nearest kinsman-redeemer had no intention of marrying her.

Boaz was certainly pleased that the way was now clear for him to marry Ruth. The two men then sealed the agreement. The nearer kinsman took off his shoe and gave it to Boaz as a symbol of the transfer of ownership.

"And the near kinsman said, 'I cannot redeem it for myself, lest I ruin my own inheritance. You redeem my right of redemption for yourself, for I cannot redeem it'" (Ruth 4:6).

The Importance of This Story

As we noted at the beginning of this chapter, the book of Ruth presents a happy picture of life in Israel during the time of the judges. In spite of the sin and warfare that is described throughout the book of Judges, there were many happy events taking place as well.

However, there is another reason that the book of Ruth has been included in the Bible. Not long after their marriage, Ruth had a son. His name was Obed. Obed became the grandfather of King David.

Not only did Ruth gain a happy marriage, but through her son she became the ancestress of Israel's royal family through David. This was a great honor, even though she could not know it at the time.

To the union of Ruth and Boaz was born Obed, then to Obed, Jesse, and to Jesse, David. Thus she also became the ancestress to the Lord Jesus Christ Himself. If you study the genealogy of Jesus in Matthew 1:5–16, you will read: "Salmon begat Boaz by Rahab, Boaz begot Obed by Ruth, Obed begot Jesse, and Jesse begot David the king. . . . And Jacob begot Joseph the husband of Mary, of whom was born Jesus who is called Christ."

INCREASE YOUR UNDERSTANDING

1. Review the story of Ruth and identify specific things that God did to bring Ruth and Boaz together.

2. The following lines are from the poem "In Heavenly Love Abiding" by Anna L. Waring.

Wherever He may guide me,
No want shall turn me back;
My Shepherd is beside me,
And nothing can I lack.
His wisdom ever walketh;
His sight is never dim.
He knows the way He taketh,
And I will walk with Him.

How does this poem illustrate the story of Ruth?

PREPARING FOR LEADERSHIP!

Responsibility is an important characteristic of good leaders. Each of the following questions addresses responsibility. Answer these questions as a review of the story of Ruth and the important role that responsibility plays in leadership.

1. How did Ruth demonstrate that she was a responsible individual?

2. What steps did Boaz take to show responsibility?

3. What responsibilities do you presently have? How have you fulfilled these responsibilities?

CHAPTER ELEVEN

The Five Remaining Minor Judges

(Judges 10:1–5; 12:8–15)

Do you remember how to determine the difference between a "major" and a "minor" judge? In Judges 3:31 you were introduced to the first minor judge, Shamgar. Shamgar is an excellent example of a minor judge. He did not lead a military deliverance and the amount of space devoted to his story in the Bible is brief.

Remember, the Bible does not place the judges into the categories of major or minor. Bible scholars have done this in order to better organize the events recorded in the book of Judges. Although a judge may be classified as minor, this does not mean that his work was unimportant.

In this chapter we will study the five remaining minor judges. Their names were Tola, Jair, Ibzan, Elon, and Abdon. Tola and Jair served

Leadership of Israel: Transition to a King

1350	1300	1250	1200	1150	1100	1050	

OTHNIEL 1377-1337

EHUD 1319-1239

GIDEON 1192-1152

ELI 1120-1080

SAMUEL 1066-1045

DEBORAH/BARAK 1239-1199

ABIMELECH 1152-1149

SAMSON 1075-1055

SHAMGAR 1260-1250

RUTH 1200-1150

IBZAN/ELON/ABDON 1080-1055

TOLA/JAIR 1149-1104

SAUL 1050-1010

JEPHTHAH 1086-1080

as judges immediately after Abimelech. Ibzan, Elon, and Abdon follow immediately after Jephthah, whom we will study in the next chapter.

There are two reasons why we study all five of these judges at the same time. First, they all served within a very short timespan. Second, the time of their work overlapped each other's. This was possible because they were serving as judges in different parts of Israel, often at the same time.

Tola (Judges 10:1–2)

Tola judged Israel for twenty-three years, the longest of any of the minor judges. Although Tola did not lead a military deliverance, in Judges 10:1 he is said to have arisen "to save Israel." If he was not a military leader, how did he save Israel?

"Wise, cautious leadership is always important. But this is especially true in times of crises."

Do you remember the trouble that Abimelech caused for the nation? Abimelech had terrorized the population during his brief three years, working terrible vengeance on the cities of Shechem and Thebez.

Bible scholars believe that after the death of Abimelech, many of the people who cooperated with him escaped to the countryside. Although Abimelech was dead, his followers were hated so much that the local people sought them out to kill them. Tola's work may have been to keep this reaction from getting out of hand and to quiet the people so that life in these two cities could once again return to normal.

Wise, cautious leadership is always important. But this is especially true in times of crises. Following Abimelech's death, there was definitely a crisis in the land. The people had been terrorized by Abimelech for so long that they became violent after his death as they sought revenge on all those who cooperated with him. People can easily overreact at such a time. Tola may well have been the one that God used to bring peace and stability during this time of turmoil.

Jair (Judges 10:3–5)

Jair served as judge for twenty-two years, one year less than Tola. Since Tola served on the west side of the Jordan and Jair on its east side, it is assumed that both of them probably served as judges at the same time. Bible scholars believe that both judges were used by God to bring stability to the land after the wicked rule of Abimelech.

Jair is one of the three minor judges who had a large family. Jair is said to have had thirty sons and that they rode on thirty donkeys. A family with thirty sons, and certainly some daughters along with them, means that the father had more than one wife. These sons controlled thirty cities.

All of this points to a kingly lifestyle similar to that practiced by Abimelech. Jair must have been a man of considerable power and authority. However, there does not seem to be any criticism of him recorded in the Bible. This means that he probably had the approval of the people who lived in the region. Jair must have been an honorable and fair man. The people followed him voluntarily.

Tola and Jair served as judges immediately following the death of Abimelech. The Bible indicates that their primary responsibility was to once again bring peace and stability to the land of Israel.

Ibzan (Judges 12:8–10)

The next three minor judges served after Jephthah. Ibzan served for seven years, Abdon for ten years, and Elon for eight years. Once again, their judgeships probably overlapped each other. Even if they did not overlap, their combined years would have totaled only twenty-five.

Since Ibzan was buried in Bethlehem, he was probably from the tribe of Judah. He is the second of the minor judges who had a large family. The Bible not only mentions his thirty sons but also his thirty daughters. The KING JAMES VERSION says that he sent his daughters "abroad" to be married and in their place he "took in thirty daughters from abroad for his sons."

BIBLE BACKGROUND
Marriage in the Old Testament

Marriage was instituted by God when He declared, "It is not good that man should be alone; I will make him a helper comparable to him" (Genesis 2:18). So God fashioned woman and brought her to man. This passage also emphasizes the truth that "a man shall leave his father and mother and be joined to his wife, and they shall become one flesh" (Genesis 2:24). This clearly teaches that God's ideal is for man to be the husband of one wife and for the marriage to be permanent.

In the Old Testament, the parents chose the mate for their son. The primary reason for this was that the bride became part of the clan. Although they were married and became "one flesh," the couple remained under the authority of the groom's father. The parents sought to choose someone who would fit into their clan and work harmoniously with her mother-in-law and sisters-in-law.

Sometimes the parents consulted with their children to see if they approved of the choice of mates being made for them. For example, Rebekah was asked if she wanted to marry Isaac (Genesis 24:58). Samson demanded that a certain girl be acquired for him. Although his parents protested, they completed the marriage contract for Samson (Judges 14:1–4).

A number of customs and steps were involved in finalizing a marriage. The first was agreeing on a price to be given to the father of the girl. The payment was compensation for the loss of a worker. The sum was mutually agreed upon. It could consist of services instead of money. For example, Jacob agreed to work for seven years for Rachel (Genesis 29:18–20). The giving and receiving of money was probably accompanied by a written agreement. After this agreement was made, the couple was considered engaged.

God's desire for his people was that they marry within the body of believers. The Mosaic law stated that an Israelite was never to marry a Canaanite. The Israelite would be constantly tempted to embrace the spouse's god as well (Exodus 34:10–17; Deuteronomy 7:3–4). Likewise, Paul commanded the members of the church at Corinth, "Do not be unequally yoked together with unbelievers" (2 Corinthians 6:14).

The word *abroad* does not necessarily mean that Ibzan sent his daughters to a foreign country or that he took in daughters from other countries for his sons. The word in the original Hebrew simply meant that he sent his daughters to other cities.

A man with this many sons and daughters was clearly a wealthy and influential man. But he must have also been a man with a well-known reputation who was interested in increasing that reputation.

By sending his thirty daughters to other cities, he was able to secure the best possible husbands for them. Certainly, these husbands would all come from fine, wealthy families. In addition, the thirty daughters-in-law that he brought in to marry his sons would also be from similar families. Ibzan was clearly a man of power, wealth, and influence. He took every opportunity to extend this power and influence.

Although Ibzan followed a kingly lifestyle and was a man of obvious family pride, God selected him to serve as one of Israel's judges. This once again reminds us that God looks upon the heart of an individual.

Elon (Judges 12:11–12)

We know very little about Elon except that he served in Zebulun near the Sea of Galilee for ten years. We are not told anything about his family or what he did.

Since he served in an area that was heavily populated by Canaanites, perhaps the influence of the Canaanites and Baal worship was increasing. The last time that Baal worship had been a problem was during the time of Gideon. God may have placed Elon there as judge to stop the increasing paganism in the area.

Although Elon is not described as a wealthy, influential man, he was obviously a man well respected by the people. There was both peace and prosperity throughout his ten-year judgeship.

Abdon (Judges 12:13–15)

Abdon was the last of the minor judges. It is clear from the mention of the forty sons and thirty grandsons that he was a wealthy man. It is interesting to note that of the five remaining minor judges, three of them lived and acted like kings. Certainly, Abimelech's influence was still being felt in the land of Israel.

Since Abdon was a judge, what were his responsibilities? Judges 12:13–15 does not provide an answer to that question. However, the answer does become clear when we realize that Abdon served as judge shortly after the death of Hophni and Phinehas.

Hophni and Phinehas, whom we will study in chapter 15, were the wicked sons of the high priest, Eli. Although they served as priests at the tabernacle, they committed terrible sins. Their wicked influence was felt throughout Israel. They eventually died at the battle of Aphek. God certainly punished them for their wickedness.

However, others copied their wicked ways. In order to stop their evil influence on other priests, God raised up Abdon as a judge during this time. We can assume that his responsibility was to put an end to the wickedness started by these two priests.

Although these minor judges are not as exciting to study as Ehud, Gideon or Samson, they had important responsibilities. God raised them up to bring peace to the land and counteract the wicked influence of the surrounding paganism.

LESSONS ON LEADERSHIP!

WISDOM IN THE MIDST OF CRISIS

A Lesson on Leadership! from Tola, Jair, Ibzan, Elon, and Abdon

Wise leadership is always important. This is particularly true in times of crises. Each of these five minor judges served during very critical times in Israel's history. Although each crisis was different, the judges responded with great wisdom.

This is an important lesson for all leaders. A crisis can be made worse if the leader overreacts or fails to listen to wise counsel. Remember, God is never taken by surprise. Even in the worst crisis, God is in control. Christian leaders need to ask God for calmness and wisdom when crises arise.

1. Tola was responsible to restore peace and order to Israel after the death of Abimelech. What types of problems did Tola face as a result of Abimelech's treatment of the people? What steps would you have taken to restore peace in the land?

2. Ibzan sought to build positive relationships with other nations and tribes through the marriages of his sons and daughters. Research examples from history in which this same marriage strategy was used to strengthen relationships between nations.

3. Choose a country that is of special interest to you and report on its marriage customs.

PREPARING FOR LEADERSHIP!

1. Many of these minor judges were wealthy and influential men. How can wealth and influence benefit a leader? How can they destroy a leader?

2. One of the responsibilities of these judges was to bring peace to the land. Maintaining peace between individuals is frequently a difficult task for leaders. Give an example of how the lack of peace between students at your school caused problems for another student or school leader.

3. Based upon the example you have just given, how was peace restored? What could the leader, or person in charge, have done to prevent the problem from happening?

CHAPTER TWELVE

Jephthah
A Costly Victory
(Judges 11:1–12:7)

In the last chapter we noted that Tola and Jair are mentioned only briefly in the first five verses of chapter 10. Although their stories are brief, forty-five years of Israel's history took place during their judgeships. Even though they may have lived at the same time, they served in widely separated parts of the country.

By now you should have a clear understanding of Israel's cycle of sin and deliverance. After Jair died, the people returned to worshiping false gods. But this time they served more heathen gods than ever before. They served the gods of Syria, of Sidon, of Moab, of Ammon, and of the Philistines.

As a result of their sin, the Lord allowed the Ammonites to punish the Israelites. The oppression the Ammonites brought upon the people was terrible. For eighteen years they inflicted severe hardship upon the nation of Israel.

Once again the Israelites cried to the Lord for deliverance. They admitted they had sinned and served false gods. Our gracious God saw that the Israelites were truly repentant; so He forgave them. The

Israel's Cycle of Sin and Deliverance

The Nation Served God — The Nation Did Evil — The Nation Forsook God — The Nation Followed Its Own Way (Pleasure) — The Nation Was Sold into Slavery (Depression and War) — The Nation in Slavery — The Nation in Servitude — The Nation Cried Out to God — The Nation Turned to God — The Nation Repented — The Nation Was Delivered — God Raised Up Judges

> "And so it was, when the people of Ammon made war against Israel, that the elders of Gilead went to get Jephthah from the land of Tob. Then they said to Jephthah, 'Come and be our commander, that we may fight against the people of Ammon.'" (Judges 11:5–6).

following story describes God's plan to deliver Israel from the Ammonites.

Jephthah, Selected by God and Men

The man God used to bring deliverance was Jephthah. The Bible records that he was the son of a harlot. In other words, he was an illegitimate son in his family. The Bible also tells us that he was treated unjustly by his half-brothers because of his birth. The situation at home became so bad that he was forced to leave. His half-brothers informed him that they would not let him share in the inheritance from their father.

Forced to leave his home, Jephthah went north to the city of Tob. While he was there he demonstrated his ability for leadership by forming a band of unemployed, adventurous men whom he molded into an effective fighting unit. He and his band of men protected cities and settlements from the Ammonites. His reputation spread throughout the northern part of Israel.

He became so well known that even the leaders in his hometown of Gilead heard of him. Although he had been forced to leave his home city of Mizpah, the town leaders traveled to Tob and asked him to return. They needed his help to combat the Ammonites in the area.

Jephthah reminded them that they had a part in forcing him to leave Gilead. He wanted to know how he could be assured that they would treat him fairly if he returned.

The elders of Gilead responded that if Jephthah would return with them to Gilead and defend the city against the Ammonites, he would be made "head over all the inhabitants of Gilead" (Judges 11:8). Of course, this promise to Jephthah was very appealing. But he made them repeat it before accepting it, just to be sure. They did and

Jephthah accompanied them back to his hometown. Upon his return, he was declared to be "head and commander over" the people in a ceremony conducted "before the Lord in Mizpah" (Judges 11:11).

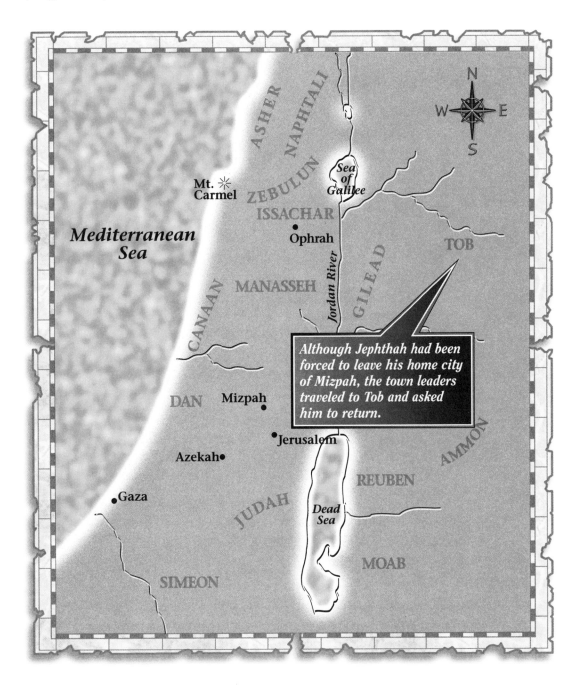

Although Jephthah had been forced to leave his home city of Mizpah, the town leaders traveled to Tob and asked him to return.

Negotiation and Then the Battle

What Jephthah did next surprised both the elders of Gilead and the Ammonites. Instead of forming an army and going right to war, he first tried to negotiate with the enemy. He tried to reason with the Ammonite ruler, clearly in an effort to avoid a battle if at all possible.

Negotiation: "to make a deal or arrange something through discussion and compromise."

Jephthah began by asking the Ammonite king why he was constantly attacking the Israelites. The king answered that it was because Israel had seized land that had belonged to Ammon at the time of the conquest.

Jephthah replied that the king's response was not true. Israel did not take land from Ammon at that time, but from Sihon, king of the Amorites. Then Jephthah reminded the king that Israel had been in possession of the land for over three hundred years. Jephthah believed that it seemed a little late for the king to now be claiming that the land belonged to the Ammonites.

No matter how strong a case Jephthah presented to the Ammonite king, he was not successful. The king was determined to fight for the land. Negotiation was over. It was now time to go to war.

Jephthah's next step was to form an army. He did this by traveling to each of the northern cities in Israel. He was looking for experienced soldiers to join his band of men. Although his army would not be large, it would consist of the finest warriors in the land.

Unlike many of the stories in the book of Judges, the Bible does not tell us about Jephthah's specific battle plan. In fact, very little about the battle is actually recorded. Whatever strategy Jephthah used, he won a complete victory. He not only won the actual battle but also drove the enemy all the way back to the Ammonite homeland. As the enemy was being pushed back, Jephthah seized as many as twenty Ammonite cities (Judges 11:33). These were the cities that the Ammonites used as fortresses for protection and bases of operation against Israel.

Thus Israel was delivered from an enemy that oppressed them for eighteen years. Ammon was so totally defeated that it no longer even controlled its vital cities. The people of Gilead, who had rejected Jephthah earlier, now recognized him as their deliverer. As promised by the elders of the city, Jephthah was recognized as judge. He remained in that position until his death, six years later.

Jephthah's Vow

Although Jephthah and his men were victorious in battle, there is another interesting event that took place during this story. It seems that before Jephthah went into battle with the Ammonites, he made a serious vow to God. Jephthah wanted to make sure that God would bless his leadership and give his army the victory. So he vowed to God, "If You will indeed deliver the people of Ammon into my hands, then it will be that whatever comes out of the doors of my house to meet me, when I return in peace from the people of Ammon, shall surely be the Lord's, and I will offer it up as a burnt offering" (Judges 11:30–31).

As we have already seen, Jephthah won a complete victory over the Ammonites. On his return home, the first one to meet him was his own daughter, who was also his only child. On seeing her and remembering the vow, Jephthah was greatly distressed. He was serious in his vow when he made it, but to carry out the vow would be very difficult. He told his daughter about the vow and that he could not go back on his promise to God.

Many Bible scholars have debated exactly how Jephthah carried out his vow. Some believe that Jephthah actually sacrificed his daughter in the form of a burnt offering. Others believe that he offered her in the sense of devoting her to the tabernacle for lifelong service.

However, most Bible scholars feel that Jephthah did not kill his daughter. If he had offered his daughter as a human sacrifice, he would have disobeyed the Mosaic law (Leviticus 18:21; 20:2–5). Second, if he sacrificed his daughter, he would have had to do so at the proper place of sacrifice, the tabernacle. No priest would have been willing to participate in that action. Finally, Judges 11:37–38 tells us that Jephthah permitted his daughter to mourn her virginity. This indicated that Jephthah offered his daughter to the Lord, thus keeping his promise; but she was not offered as a human sacrifice. Instead she would remain unmarried and serve the Lord in the temple for the rest of her life.

> *"Again, you shall say to the children of Israel: 'Whoever of the children of Israel, or of the strangers who sojourn in Israel, who gives any of his descendants to Molech, he shall surely be put to death. The people of the land shall stone him with stones. I will set My face against that man, and will cut him off from his people, because he has given some of his descendants to Molech, to defile My sanctuary and profane My holy name' "*
> *(Leviticus 20:2–3).*

This event in Jephthah's life is a clear reminder that we should not make hasty promises. When a promise is made, whether to God or to man, it should be kept. When we fail to keep our promises, it is a reflection upon our character. Those who make promises that are not kept cannot be trusted. We must be careful when we make a vow. As Christians, we must always fulfill the promises that we make.

LESSONS ON LEADERSHIP!

AVOID CONFLICT WHENEVER POSSIBLE

Jephthah's Lesson on Leadership!

Jephthah's attempt to negotiate with the Ammonite king is an important *Lesson on Leadership!* Although he was a man of war, he tried to avoid war by talking through the problem with his enemy.

It would have been very natural for Jephthah, out of personal pride, to have wanted to show off before the people of his hometown. After the way they treated him, he would have liked to show them what a good warrior he was. But Jephthah did not let his personal pride get in the way of doing what was right. He first tried to negotiate a peaceful settlement to avoid bloodshed. It is always better to talk about differences than to fight about them!

INCREASE YOUR UNDERSTANDING

1. From the book of Proverbs, identify verses that teach us to use kind words to avoid conflict with others.

2. How would you characterize someone who is a good negotiator?

3. Research the practice of human sacrifice by pagan religions. What does the Bible say about those who practice human sacrifice?

4. Most Bible scholars believe that Jephthah's daughter spent the remainder of her life serving the Lord in the tabernacle. What types of responsibilities would she have had?

PREPARING FOR LEADERSHIP!

If we are to be effective leaders, our relationships with others must be characterized by godliness, trust, and honesty. Respond to each of the following questions as they relate to these three characteristics.

Godliness: Our speech reveals our character. If we talk like the world, people will think we are of the world. Can your friends tell by your speech that you are a Christian? What are some identifying marks of a Christian's speech?

Trust: Have you ever heard someone say, "Promises are made to be broken"? In God's eyes, promises should never be broken. What types of promises do people most often break?

Honesty: Has anyone ever offended you? How did you respond? In Matthew 18:15–17, Jesus told us to go directly to that person to resolve the problem. Why is this approach to solving problems with others important for a Christian leader?

CHAPTER THIRTEEN

Samson

His Birth and Separation unto the Lord

(Judges 13, 14)

The next two chapters consider the life and judgeship of Samson, probably the most well known of all of the judges. This chapter will focus on his birth and the Nazirite vow. In the next chapter, we will consider his exploits and ultimate victory over the Philistines.

From Judges 13:1, we learn that the nation of Israel was once again nearing the end of another cycle of sin and deliverance. The people sinned and God delivered them over to their enemy. This time God delivered them into the hands of the Philistines. The Philistines had come into the land of Israel during the forty-year period of peace following Deborah's victory over the Canaanites. It was now approximately one hundred years later, and the Philistines had become firmly established in the land.

The objective the Philistines had for the nation of Israel was quite different from those of the other oppressing nations. The other nations wanted to simply rob Israel of its crops and flocks. The Philistines actually wanted to take over the country in order to live there.

The Philistines were strong and ruthless warriors. They would not allow anyone to stand in the way of getting what they wanted. At the time of

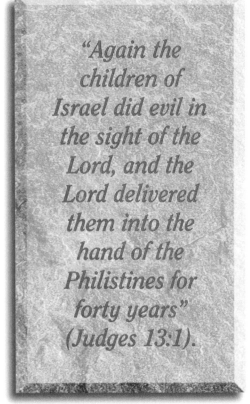

"Again the children of Israel did evil in the sight of the Lord, and the Lord delivered them into the hand of the Philistines for forty years" *(Judges 13:1).*

Samson, the Philistines had already controlled Israel for forty years. This was the longest of any oppression. God was about to send the newest of his daring deliverers, the man Samson.

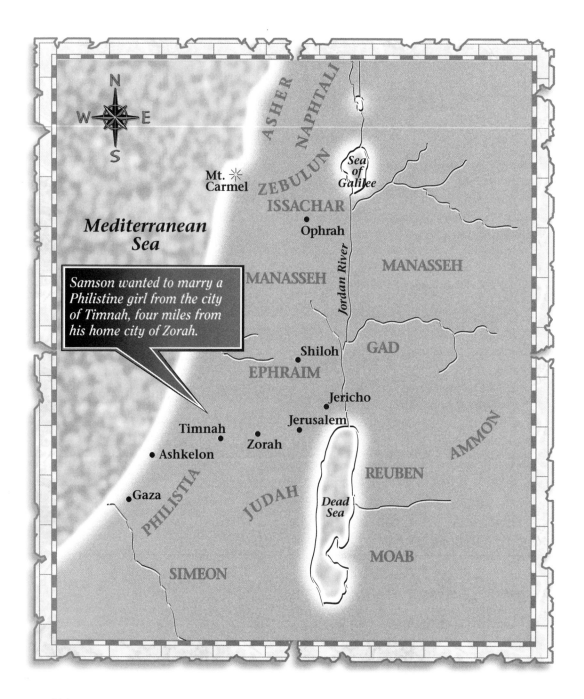

Samson wanted to marry a Philistine girl from the city of Timnah, four miles from his home city of Zorah.

The Announcement of Samson's Birth

The story of Samson begins with a detailed description of the supernatural announcement of his birth. This is a unique event in the book of Judges. Nothing is mentioned at all regarding the births of the other judges, except that Jephthah was born illegitimately.

Samson's parents lived in the city of Zorah, near the dividing line between Philistine and Israelite territory. His father's name was Manoah. One day the angel of the Lord appeared to Manoah's wife and announced that she would have a son. This was startling news for her. She was certainly surprised that the angel of the Lord appeared to her. But she was also surprised to learn that she would have a son because she had been barren for many years.

In addition to announcing the birth of her son, the angel of the Lord also told her to be careful not to drink wine or strong drink or eat anything unclean, because the child to be born would be a Nazirite to God. Then the angel gave the most important news of all. This son would "begin to deliver Israel out of the hand of the Philistines" (Judges 13:5).

The woman quickly went to tell this exciting news to her husband, Manoah. Upon hearing the news, Manoah doubted that his wife had actually seen an angel. So he asked the Lord to send the angel to them again and tell them more about this promised son.

Manoah's prayer was answered and the angel returned. However, the angel did not give them any additional news. After repeating the promise given to Manoah's wife, the angel of the Lord miraculously disappeared in the smoke of the offering prepared by Manoah for the occasion. Manoah then recognized that this was the angel of the Lord. From that time forward, they looked forward to the birth of their son.

Samson Was to Be a Nazirite

The angel of the Lord clearly told Manoah's wife that Samson should be a Nazirite "from the womb" (Judges 13:5). This meant that, while she was pregnant, she could not drink wine or strong drink and could not eat anything unclean. These were requirements that were normally imposed only on the one who took the Nazirite vow.

What was the Nazirite vow? The Nazirite vow is described in Numbers 6:1–8. This pattern of life was normally entered into only for a short time. The person would take the vow of the Nazirite and then drink no form of strong drink, consume nothing made from the product of the vine, refrain from cutting his hair, and make sure that he never came near a dead body.

> *"Then the Lord spoke to Moses, saying, 'Speak to the children of Israel, and say to them: "When either a man or woman consecrates an offering to take the vow of a Nazirite, to separate himself to the Lord, he shall separate himself from wine and similar drink; he shall drink neither vinegar made from wine nor vinegar made from similar drink; neither shall he drink any grape juice, nor eat fresh grapes or raisins. All the days of his separation he shall eat nothing that is produced by the grapevine, from seed to skin. All the days of the vow of his separation no razor shall come upon his head; until the days are fulfilled for which he separated himself to the Lord, he shall be holy. Then he shall let the locks of the hair of his head grow. All the days that he separates himself to the Lord he shall not go near a dead body. He shall not make himself unclean even for his father or his mother, for his brother or his sister, when they die, because his separation to God is on his head. All the days of his separation he shall be holy to the Lord" ' "* (Numbers 6:1–8).

BIBLE BACKGROUND

Nazirite Vow

The word *nazirite* means to "separate" or "consecrate." It describes a person who took a vow to separate from certain worldly things and to consecrate himself to God. Anyone among the Hebrew people could take this vow; there were no restrictions as in the case of the priest. Rich or poor, man or woman, master or slave—all were free to become Nazirites.

Nazirites did not withdraw from society and live as hermits; however, they did agree to follow certain regulations for a specified time. While no number of days for the vow is given in the Old Testament, Jewish tradition prescribed thirty days. Samson, Samuel, and John the Baptist were the only "Nazirites for life" recorded in the Bible. Before they were born, their vows were taken for them by their parents.

If an individual accidentally broke his Nazirite vow, he had to undergo a ceremony of restoration for cleansing (Numbers 6:9–12). He shaved his head, brought two turtledoves or two pigeons to the priest for offerings, and the priest made atonement for him. In addition, a Nazirite had to present a lamb for a trespass offering. It was as if he was starting all over again and the days already served under the vow did not count.

The Nazirite vow was a part of the old law and is not imposed on today's Christians. But because it was personal and voluntary, we do have much to learn from this Old Testament practice. God wants us to live a separated, holy life and to abstain from things of the world. Christians must be dedicated to God's service not just for thirty days, but for life.

The purpose of the vow was to indicate a complete dedication to God. It was an outward testimony to the entire community that this person was fully committed to serving God. When the angel of the

Lord indicated that Samson was to be a Nazirite all of his life, the angel was saying that Samson should be a truly dedicated person all the days he lived. As the story of Samson unfolds, we will see that Samson did quite well for much of his life. However, in the last days of his life he committed serious sin.

The reason that God imposed this lifelong requirement on Samson was obvious. Samson would be seen as a living miracle of God's power to deliver His people. He would be given greater physical strength than any other man who had ever lived. God was extending to Samson a great privilege. He would have to remain humble and recognize that his unique gift was to be used only for the glory of God. Both the Israelites and the Philistines would know that God was the true source of Samson's strength.

The First Encounter between Samson and the Philistines

When Samson reached an appropriate age, the Spirit of the Lord came upon him. Up until that time, Samson was probably like any other young man. But now things changed. The Spirit of the Lord had come upon him to impart this miraculous strength. Bible scholars believe that Samson was probably eighteen or nineteen years old when he received this special strength from the Lord. Although we are not told exactly how or when this took place, it was certainly a day that Samson would never forget.

The first time that the Bible records that Samson used this strength was at his marriage to a Philistine girl. Samson was probably about twenty years old at the time. Although the Bible does not explain how they met, we do know that she was from the city of Timnah, about four miles from Samson's home city of Zorah.

He immediately fell in love with her and asked his parents to arrange the wedding for him. It was a common practice for parents to make the wedding arrangements for their children. However, since she was not an Israelite, his parents refused to honor his request. The Mosaic law (Deuteronomy 7:3–4) did not allow intermarriage. But Samson insisted and his parents finally agreed to do as he had asked.

Although Samson had a wedding on his mind, God had another reason for allowing this intermarriage to take place. According to

Judges 14:4, the wedding was to provide "an occasion to move against the Philistines" by which a quarrel could be provoked. In other words, the wedding was to be the first instance when Samson would use his divinely given strength to carry out his Philistine assignment.

On his way to Timnah with his parents to arrange the wedding, Samson met and killed a young lion with his bare hands. Many days later, when he was once again traveling the same road to Timnah, he saw the dried-up carcass of the lion he had previously killed. This time, he noticed that a swarm of bees had made a hive in the carcass.

As the wedding day approached, Samson was celebrating with thirty of his special friends. In the midst of the celebration, he told a riddle based upon what he had seen. Riddles were a common form of entertainment in those days. Samson presented his riddle to his companions saying, "Out of the eater came something to eat, and out of the strong came something sweet" (Judges 14:14). He told his companions that if they could solve the riddle during the week of feasting prior to the wedding, he would give them thirty changes of clothing, but if they could not, then they would owe him thirty changes of clothing.

"Nor shall you make marriages with them. You shall not give your daughter to their son, nor take their daughter for your son. For they will turn your sons away from following Me, to serve other gods; so the anger of the Lord will be aroused against you and destroy you suddenly" (Deuteronomy 7:3–4).

No matter how hard they tried, the thirty companions could not solve the riddle. Finally, on the seventh and last day of the feast, the companions forced Samson's bride to get the answer for them. Through trickery and tears, she was able to get Samson to tell her the answer to his riddle. Immediately, she told the answer to the Philistine companions and they won the contest.

Samson knew that he had been tricked. He went to the Philistine port city of Ashkelon, about twenty-four miles from Timnah, and killed thirty Philistines. He took their garments from them and gave them to the thirty Philistine companions to pay off his bet.

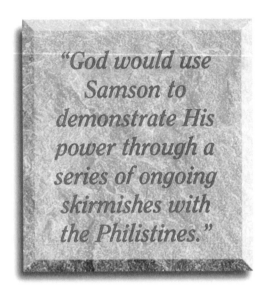

"God would use Samson to demonstrate His power through a series of ongoing skirmishes with the Philistines."

Samson was so angry at how he had been tricked, he left his young bride in Timnah and returned home to Zorah. The Bible records that the bride's father then gave her to one of the thirty companions as his wife.

This story of the wedding is an illustration of the task God had given to Samson. It was not God's plan for Samson to raise up an army and fight the Philistines at one specific time. Actually, Samson would be a thorn in the flesh of the Philistines for many years to come. Samson would begin a process of deliverance that would be completed by someone else. God would use Samson to demonstrate His power through a series of ongoing skirmishes with the Philistines.

Samson's Unlearned Lesson

A lesson Samson should have learned from this occasion, and did not, was that the Philistines could not be trusted. The thirty companions who were supposed to be his special friends throughout the wedding festivities turned against him by forcing his bride to discover and share the secret of his riddle. His bride was even an accomplice to the deceit. If the bride would have been a true wife, she would have shared the threat of the thirty men with Samson and then done everything possible to protect herself and her father's house. Samson, with the great strength he possessed, could have certainly protected them.

Samson did not understand that the Philistines could not be trusted. Many years later, when he met Delilah, he would fall into the same trap again.

FAILURE TO DO WHAT'S RIGHT BRINGS DISASTER

Samson's Lesson on Leadership!

Samson knew that it was wrong to marry a Philistine woman. Although his parents tried to stop him, he demanded his own way. As a result of his disobedience and compromise, he caused the death of thirty innocent men.

Before the story of Samson ends, we will once again learn that his sin of compromise and disobedience will not only destroy his ability to lead, but will ultimately take his life.

As leaders, our words and actions are carefully watched by others. We must be especially careful to always do what's right. Our position as a leader does not justify disobedience or compromise.

INCREASE YOUR UNDERSTANDING

1. The angel of the Lord warned Samson's mother not to drink wine or eat anything unclean because her son would be a Nazirite to God. What is "unclean" food? Why did God declare certain foods to be "unclean"?

2. There is considerable controversy as to the identity of the angel of the Lord. Research this controversy and then explain the position you have taken as to who the angel of the Lord is.

3. Compare the ceremony and festivities of an Old Testament wedding to a wedding today. Identify both differences and similarities.

PREPARING FOR LEADERSHIP!

Although Samson was chosen by God to deliver Israel and given miraculous strength to carry out the task, he disobeyed God by desiring to marry the Philistine woman. His willingness to compromise doing what was right would lead to disaster in his life.

When we compromise what we know to be right, we can be assured of serious consequences. What are the consequences of compromise in each of the following areas?

Area of Compromise

Dating Someone Who Is Not a Christian

Consequence

Area of Compromise

Developing Close Friendships with Unbelievers

Consequence

Area of Compromise

Not Attending Bible Study and Church

Consequence

Area of Compromise

Failing to Read the Bible and Pray on a Regular Basis

Consequence

CHAPTER FOURTEEN

Samson
His Exploits and Dramatic Exit
(Judges 15, 16)

Although Samson was supposed to live a life that was dedicated to God, he continued to compromise with the world. However, in spite of his disobedience, God continued to use him to deliver Israel from the hands of the Philistines.

As last week's lesson ended, Samson returned to his home city in anger. Meanwhile, the father of his Philistine bride gave her in marriage to one of the thirty companions who deceived Samson. Since Samson went home and his bride married someone else, you probably thought that this story had ended. Wrong! This story is far from over!

Samson Returns to Timnah

At the time of the wheat harvest, Samson returned to claim the bride he deserted. No one knows exactly how much time passed since he left Timnah in anger and his bride married someone else. It was probably less than a year, yet long enough for his anger to cool down.

When he arrived, he was met by the father of the woman he was supposed to have wed. The father informed Samson that she had been given to one of his former companions. The father encouraged Samson to marry one of his younger daughters. But Samson refused. His next step was to get revenge.

Since it was the time for harvest, Samson decided to attack the Philistines in a way that would hurt them the most. He knew they were dependent upon their wheat to provide them with enough food for the rest of the year. He caught three hundred foxes, tied firebrands to pairs of them joined by their tails, and released them to run through the Philistine grainfields, vineyards, and olive orchards. Tying the animals together assured that they would not run and try to hide in their holes. Instead, the foxes ran wildly through the land setting fire everywhere they went.

In response, the angry neighbors of the bride's father blamed him for Samson's actions. They stormed the father's house and burned both the father and the girl. Samson was so angered by what the neighbors did, he attacked the Philistines. The Bible records that many Philistines died by his hand.

The Philistines Pursue Samson

Knowing that the Philistines would follow him, Samson did not go directly home. Instead, he "dwelt in the cleft of the rock of Etam." The Philistines, having been sorely defeated by Samson, were not going to stand idly by. They pursued him into the land of Judah.

As the Philistines arrived, the men of Judah approached them and asked them why they had come. The Philistines responded that they came to get Samson.

> *"Do you not know that the Philistines rule over us? What is this you have done to us?" (Judges 15:11).*

Because the people of Judah were so afraid of the Philistines, they went to Samson to try to convince him to turn himself in. Their words to Samson must have been hard for him to understand. Instead of thanking Samson for his brave deeds, they actually blamed him for bringing what they thought was possible danger on them.

Then they informed Samson that they had come to bind him and deliver him to the Philistines. Samson did not want to endanger his countrymen, so he said he would permit them to bind him if they would agree not to attack him themselves. Samson knew that if they attacked him he would be forced to defend himself. They agreed and he submitted himself to them as they bound him with new ropes and led him away to the Philistines.

When he was brought to where the Philistines were camped, he once again demonstrated the power that the Lord had given to him. Samson broke the new ropes that bound him, picked up the jawbone of a donkey, and killed one thousand Philistine soldiers.

God's Word records that Samson ruled over the nation of Israel for nearly twenty years, protecting them from the Philistines. During these years Samson may have carried on some anti-Philistine activities, but the Bible tells us very little about what happened during this twenty-year judgeship.

Samson's Sin with Delilah

The story of Samson and Delilah is one of the most often-told stories in the Bible. Delilah was a scheming Philistine woman. She lived in the Valley of Sorek, not far from Samson's place of birth, Zorah. Delilah was not described as a harlot, but certainly her moral standards were very low.

It did not take long for the Philistines to learn of Samson's regular visits to see Delilah. Seeing an opportunity to defeat Samson, the Philistine leaders came to Delilah for help. They offered her the large sum of eleven hundred pieces of silver if

BIBLE BACKGROUND

Money in the Old Testament

Before the use of any form of currency, a system of barter—or trading of property—was the common form of payment for goods or services. In Old Testament times, land itself became an immediate asset because it was a possession that could be traded. But produce and especially livestock were more convenient because they could be moved so easily.

Grain, oil, and wine were also used in bartering. King Solomon traded wheat and olive oil for the cedar and cypress trees needed to build the temple (1 Kings 5:10–11). The Israelites were taxed in the amount of one-tenth of their grain or wine (1 Samuel 8:15).

Soon metals began to replace goods and services as items of exchange. Silver and gold became popular forms of money because copper and bronze were in demand for weapons. In fact, silver was so commonly used as money that the Hebrew word for silver came to mean money.

Eventually pieces of metal were standardized, then stamped to designate their weight and value. Bankers who exchanged one nation's currency, or one size of coin, for another were called "money changers." These people provided a convenience, charging a fee for their services.

Samson's Falsehoods

Three times Samson told Delilah falsehoods. He said that he would become weak if . . .

. . . he was bound with seven moist bowstrings

. . . he was tied with new, unused ropes

. . . seven locks of his hair were woven together and fastened with a pin.

she would learn and tell them the secret of Samson's strength. She agreed, demonstrating that she loved money more than Samson.

Time after time, Delilah tried to learn the secret of Samson's strength. At first Samson was able to resist her requests. Three times he told her falsehoods: first, that he would become weak if he was bound with seven moist bowstrings; second, that he would become weak if he was tied with new, unused ropes; and third, that he would become weak if the seven locks of his hair were woven together and fastened with a pin.

Each time Samson told a falsehood, Delilah had someone come and do to Samson the action he had described. But Samson never lost any of his strength. It should have been clear to Samson that Delilah did not really love him but was only interested in seeing him captured. But, if Samson did realize her true intent, he did not do anything about it.

Finally, Samson told her the truth. He told her that he had been a Nazirite all his life. If the hair of his head were cut off, he would be as weak as other men. Delilah summoned the Philistine leaders. She cut off Samson's hair as he slept. The Philistines then seized him and found that he was helpless. Samson's vow had been broken. God had now removed his power.

Samson's Final Exit

The Philistines were victorious. They now had captured Samson. They took him from Delilah's house, put out his eyes, brought him to Gaza, bound him in brass chains, and put him to work in the prison house grinding grain. The Philistines wanted to humiliate Samson by reducing him to a crippled slave.

Samson's disobedient life not only brought him personal shame but it also brought reproach to the God of Israel. The Philistines knew that Samson was God's chosen servant. When they captured Samson, they had a twofold reason for rejoicing. Not only had they taken Samson as prisoner, the one who had slain so many of their people; but they also demonstrated that their god, Dagon, was more powerful than the God of Israel. Thus they rejoiced and sacrificed to Dagon because Samson had become their slave.

Samson's imprisonment provides a clear picture of the consequences of sin. His prison was real. It was a foul-smelling dungeon by night and an unending place of grinding grain during the day. His eyes were gone and his body bound. Since he had caused so much suffering for the Philistines, they were sure to make his imprisonment as miserable as possible.

In spite of all of the punishment the Philistines had brought upon Samson, they wanted to punish him even more. They took him to the temple of Dagon, set him between two pillars and mocked him publicly. This was certainly a great day of victory for the Philistines. The temple was filled with people who had come to worship Dagon and see Samson disgraced.

Yet Samson's life was not over. Once again, he turned back to God and sought His help. Samson's final words to God reveal his brokenness and sorrow for his sin.

First of all, he called upon the Lord to remember him. He knew that he had sinned and that God had turned him over to the Philistines. Next, he asked the Lord to strengthen him. Samson knew that his strength was not of himself but was from God. Finally, he desired to bring death to the Philistines and die with them. He knew that his sin must be punished.

BIBLE BACKGROUND

Dagon

Dagon was the chief god of the ancient Philistines, a grain and fertility god whose most famous temples were at Gaza and Ashdod. Ancient texts indicate that Dagon was a very ancient god. These texts show that Dagon was being worshiped before Abraham entered Canaan about 2000 B.C. Dagon continued to be worshiped by the Canaanites up to the time of Christ.

God granted Samson's final request. God returned Samson's strength to him and he was able to dislodge the two central supporting columns of the temple from their bases. As the supporting columns came crashing to the ground, so did the rest of the temple. By destroying the temple in this way, Samson killed more of the enemy in this time of his own death than in all his prior years.

Samson's Attitude toward Sin

Throughout most of his life, Samson did not understand the serious consequences of committing sin. This becomes very clear when we compare Samson's attitude toward sin with the attitude demonstrated by Joseph.

Joseph was faced with a situation similar to that of Samson. Joseph knew that God had a special plan for him. So did Samson. Joseph was faced with an immoral temptation. So was Samson. Joseph brought deliverance for his people from famine. Samson brought deliverance for his people from the Philistines. Joseph realized that he could interpret dreams through the power of God. Samson realized that his strength was from God. Both of these men had much in common, and both of them were used by God.

Although there is much similarity in the lives of the two men, their attitude toward sin made all the difference in their lives. When Joseph was given the opportunity to sin, he fled. Although he experienced hardship for a brief time, he was eventually made ruler over Egypt, married, was reunited with his family, brought deliverance from famine for his people, and met a peaceful death.

Samson yielded to his temptation. His weakness not only caused him to commit the same sin again but also caused him to commit murder, break his Nazirite vow, be

Similarities of Joseph and Samson

- *Both knew that God had a special plan for them.*

- *Joseph brought deliverance from famine; Samson brought deliverance from the Philistines.*

- *God gave Joseph the power to interpret dreams and Samson his great strength.*

captured, lose his sight, and finally lose his life. The final days of Samson's life are a clear illustration of Romans 6:23, "For the wages of sin is death."

GOD GIVES US TALENTS FOR USE IN HIS SERVICE

Samson's Second Lesson on Leadership!

The superhuman strength that God gave Samson was to be used to deliver the nation of Israel from the hands of the Philistines. Although Samson did use his strength to carry out God's assignment, Samson also used his strength for selfish purposes.

What special talents, or abilities, has God given to you? God expects us to use the talents He has given us to serve Him. If we fail to give God the glory for the talents He has given us, we can be assured that God will never totally bless our lives or our leadership for Him.

INCREASE YOUR UNDERSTANDING

1. Prepare a map that shows the location of all of the judges you have studied.

2. Delilah repeatedly betrayed Samson to the Philistines. Do you think Samson was aware of what she was doing? If so, why do you think he told her the secret of his strength?

3. Review the story of Joseph as recorded in Genesis 39. Develop a chart that shows the similarities and differences between the stories of Joseph and Potiphar's wife and Samson and Delilah.

PREPARING FOR LEADERSHIP!

1. Make a list of the talents, or abilities, that you believe God has given to you.

   (a)

   (b)

   (c)

   (d)

   (e)

2. Now that you have completed your list, answer the following questions:

   (a) How can these talents, or abilities, be used to serve God?

   (b) How can these talents, or abilities, make you a more effective Christian leader?

DARING DELIVERERS

CHAPTER FIFTEEN

Eli

A Godly Servant during Evil Days

(1 Samuel 1, 2)

Difficult days call for great men. Often God gives His greatest gifts to those who lead when times are the most difficult. This was certainly true in the closing days of the judges. Samson is just one example of a great man who was given great strength to accomplish the task set before him. God also blessed two other outstanding men, Eli and Samuel.

You might be asking yourself right now, "Why are we studying Eli and Samuel? I thought Samson was the last judge." Although Samson was the last of the judges to deliver the nation of Israel from a foreign oppressor, many Bible scholars consider Samuel to actually be the last of the judges to serve in a ruling capacity. It was after the ministry of Samuel that Israel crowned its first king, Saul. The period of the judges officially ended when Saul became king.

However, in order to fully understand Samuel's ministry, we must begin with Eli. Eli had become high priest at the age of fifty-eight. As the story of Samuel opens (1 Samuel 1), Eli is now past the age of seventy. These last few years of Eli's life were very important. He would not only witness Samuel's birth and call to ministry but he would also witness the destruction of his two wicked sons. Eli's life and ministry hold many valuable lessons for each of us.

Eli Becomes a Spiritual Father to Samuel

One day Eli was conducting his normal tabernacle duties when he noticed Hannah praying. He noticed that although she was praying silently, her lips were moving. At first he thought she might be drunk. But, when he questioned her, she said she was praying earnestly for a son. Eli was so touched by her desire for a son that he gave his blessing to her.

> *"Now Hannah spoke in her heart; only her lips moved, but her voice was not heard. Therefore Eli thought she was drunk"*
> *(1 Samuel 1:13).*

In her prayer, Hannah promised that if God would give her a son, she would in turn give the child back to God as a tabernacle priest. This was a promise similar to the one given by Jephthah with his daughter many years before. In addition to Hannah's promise to give her son back to the Lord, she promised that he would be a Nazirite, in the pattern of Samson, not letting a razor "come upon his head" (1 Samuel 1:11).

God graciously granted her request. When Samuel was born, Hannah remembered and kept her promise. Although this must have been very difficult for her to do, she brought him to the tabernacle and presented him to Eli. The Bible does not record any other example of a male individual being given to the tabernacle in this way. Since Samuel would no longer live at home, Eli became his "spiritual father." This was a unique responsibility for Eli.

Eli and His Two Sons

As high priest, Eli would carry out the customary responsibilities. He would conduct ceremonies, offer prayers, and give instruction to other priests and the people. Eli was a godly man. The Bible speaks of his compassion, submission to God's authority, and respect for God's Law.

However, Eli had made one major mistake. His failure was in the rearing of his two sons, Hophni and Phinehas. Both young men turned out to be very sinful in the conduct of their priestly responsibilities. Their sins were mainly in two areas. First, they perverted the sacrifices. They kept more than their proper share of what the people brought to sacrifice. Second, they participated in immoral conduct with some of the women who served at the tabernacle. This group of women was probably composed of young ladies, like Jephthah's daughter, who had devoted their lives for tabernacle service.

Although Eli spoke to his sons about these sins, he did not apply sufficient discipline to stop their sinful behavior. Thus God held Eli, as well as his sons, accountable for their actions.

Because God held Eli responsible for the sins of his sons, He sent a warning to Eli on two different occasions. The first warning came through a person called merely a "man of God," who was probably a prophet of the day. The second warning came through Samuel.

The warning from the "man of God" was clear and direct. Because Eli did not stop the sins of his sons, punishment would now come upon Eli's house. First, Eli's house would be destroyed. No longer would any member of his family serve as a high priest. Also, both of Eli's own sons would die in one day.

The second warning came through the young man, Samuel. It obviously came at a later time from the first warning because the sins of Eli's sons had gotten much worse. Through Samuel, God reminded Eli

BIBLE BACKGROUND

The High Priest

The high priest was both the chief priest and supreme civil leader of the people of Israel. Although the office of high priest was hereditary, its holder had to be without physical defect as well as holy in conduct (Leviticus 21:5–8). He could marry only a "virgin of his own people" (Leviticus 21:14) or a believer in God. His wife could not be a widow, a divorced woman, or an impure woman.

A high priest was consecrated (installed in office) by an elaborate seven-day service at the tabernacle or temple (Exodus 29; Leviticus 8). The high priest's special dress represented his function as mediator between God and man.

The most important responsibility of the high priest was to conduct the service on the Day of Atonement, the tenth day of the seventh month each year. On this day, he alone entered the Holy Place inside the veil before God. Having made sacrifice for himself and for the people, he brought the blood into the Holy of Holies and sprinkled it on the mercy seat, "God's throne." This he did to make atonement for himself and the people for all their sins committed during the year that just ended (Exodus 30:10; Leviticus 16). Jesus' ministry as High Priest in the New Testament is compared with this particular service (Hebrews 9:1–28).

that the punishment outlined by the "man of God" would indeed come true. Eli had been given every opportunity to deal with the sins of his sons. Now God would execute punishment upon Eli and his sons because of their sins.

The punishment was carried out just as the "man of God" had predicted. Abiathar, Eli's descendant, should have been the next high priest. However, during the time of Solomon, he was replaced by Zadok. Hophni and Phinehas, Eli's two sons, were killed on the same day during the battle of Aphek. Both Eli and his sons paid the price for their sins.

Eli and the Priesthood

The most important reason for studying Eli is to understand his relationship to Samuel. It is through a study of the life of Eli that we also learn about what is happening among the priests during this time. A study of Eli's life gives us a picture of the spiritual conditions throughout Israel.

The Sins of Hophni and Phinehas

- *They perverted the sacrifices.*

- *They participated in immoral conduct with some of the women who served in the tabernacle.*

The seriousness of the sins of Hophni and Phinehas, the sons of the high priest, provide a glimpse of how some of Israel's spiritual leaders abused their positions. They not only stole from the sacrifices offered to God in the tabernacle but they also committed sexual sins with the women serving at the tabernacle. Their sins were so serious that "the Lord desired to kill them" (1 Samuel 2:25).

But Hophni and Phinehas were not the only priests who committed sins. The Bible indicated that similar sins were being committed by other priests throughout the country. If the religious leaders were regularly committing sins, what would the effect be on the average person? It is no wonder that there was so much sin throughout the land of Israel during the closing days of the judges.

If you were to study Israel's overall history, you would note that the nation experienced many dark days. There were certain periods when conditions within the land were terrible for the people. One of these periods, and maybe the worst of them all, was here at the close of the time of the judges. The sins of Hophni and Phinehas, which were typical of the priesthood in general, probably took place during the lowest point in Israel's history.

All this means that there was a great need for a man like Samuel to arise as leader. There was a need to stop the rapid growth of sin. There was a need for a shepherd who could give some sense of security to the nation. There was a need to stir renewed interest among the priests and Levites to perform their ministry. There was a need to bring a spiritual revival so that God would provide a full deliverance from the Philistines. There was a need to do so much, yet there did not seem to be anyone who would accept the responsibility to change the direction of a nation. God prepared a special man for these difficult days. In the next two chapters we will learn more about this special servant of God, Samuel.

Israel Had Many Needs

. . . *a need to stop the rapid growth of sin*

. . . *a need for a shepherd who could give some sense of security to the nation*

. . . *a need to stir renewed interest among the priests and Levites to perform their ministry*

. . . *a need to bring a spiritual revival.*

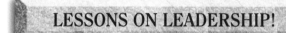

LESSONS ON LEADERSHIP!

THE IMPORTANCE OF PARENTAL RESPONSIBILITY

Eli's Lesson on Leadership!

God held Eli accountable for the sinful behavior of his two sons. Certainly, the best time for Eli to have disciplined his sons was when the boys were growing up. By the time of their mention in this story, they were already adults and their behavior patterns set. But even as adults, Eli still had the authority to stop their evil acts.

This is an important lesson for every parent, especially those who serve in positions of leadership. The task of rearing children is extremely important. Even the work of God—such as being a high priest—is not an excuse for neglecting this important responsibility.

INCREASE YOUR UNDERSTANDING

1. Identify the major sacrifices described in the Old Testament. What was the significance of each of these sacrifices?

2. Explain how the ministry of the high priest is similar to Jesus' ministry as our High Priest.

3. Research the battle of Aphek. Identify who fought in the battle as well as the reasons for the battle. Explain how Hophni and Phinehas died.

PREPARING FOR LEADERSHIP!

The priests, during Eli's days, provided a very poor spiritual example for the people of Israel. Because of the sinful testimony of the priests, idolatry and wickedness were common throughout the land.

Even though God has not yet called you to a position of leadership, as a Christian you have a responsibility to maintain a godly testimony. Make a list of specific things that you can do right now to communicate a positive, godly testimony to your family and friends.

What I Can Do to Communicate a Positive, Godly Testimony to My Family and Friends?

1.

2.

3.

4.

5.

CHAPTER SIXTEEN

Samuel

Twenty Years of Ministry

(1 Samuel 3–7)

As we conclude our study of the judges, we turn to one of the most outstanding people of the Old Testament. Samuel was God's man for one of Israel's most crucial hours. He performed tasks of major significance. He stepped into a position which presented discouraging obstacles, and he moved ahead in spite of them to accomplish what few would have believed possible.

Preparation is always important for effective leadership. A person must be qualified for what he or she is to do. Samuel's preparation was uniquely arranged by God. It equipped him in just the right way to step into the demanding work God had in mind for him.

The Story of Samuel's Preparation

In the last chapter, the story of Samuel's birth was told. After Samuel was born, Hannah kept her promise and brought him to Eli at the tabernacle. Although Samuel did not live at home, Hannah was able to see him regularly. Each time she visited him, she brought him "a little robe" (1 Samuel 2:19).

Samuel's education had to be conducted at the tabernacle. Normally, education took place at home with the parents as the

> *"Only take heed to yourself, and diligently keep yourself, lest you forget the things your eyes have seen, and lest they depart from your heart all the days of your life. And teach them to your children and your grandchildren"* (Deuteronomy 4:9).

teachers. Their primary responsibility was to teach their children the Law of God (Deuteronomy 4:9). In Samuel's case, however, the task had to be assumed by people at the tabernacle. Eli, of course, was the one primarily responsible for Samuel's education. The Bible reveals that Samuel soon developed a deep love and respect for Eli.

Since Samuel lived at the central sanctuary, he was able to gain a firsthand understanding of what it meant to worship God. He grew up with the experience of seeing sacrifices and offerings presented every day. He did not have to learn about them merely from the lips of a parent in a distant city, but was able to see them in actual practice directly before his eyes.

Samuel also had the opportunity to actually read and study the Law of God. Unlike today, copies of God's Word were only available in places of worship. Samuel had the advantage of being educated at the place where these copies were kept. He also had as his teacher the man who knew the Law of God better than anyone else.

Because Samuel lived at the tabernacle, he also had a firsthand knowledge of the sinful conditions in the land. The tabernacle was the place where the priests and Levites discussed the spiritual conditions of the people. Besides this, Samuel

BIBLE BACKGROUND

Tabernacle

The tabernacle served as a place of worship for the nation of Israel during its early history. On Mount Sinai, after the Lord had given the commandments to Moses, He instructed Moses to construct the tabernacle. This was to be a center for worship and place where the people could focus upon the presence of the Lord.

The tabernacle was divided into two rooms; the Holy Place and the Holy of Holies. In the Holy of Holies was the ark of the covenant, the holiest item in the tabernacle. The ark contained a copy of the stone tablet with the Ten Commandments, a copy of the entire Law of Moses, a gold pot filled with manna, and Aaron's rod that budded.

Responsibilities for the care and moving of the tabernacle were delegated to various families of the tribe of Levi. As the years passed, certain other structures were added to the tabernacle. These included living quarters for the priests and Levites who served there. By the end of the period of the judges, during the time of Eli, some of the attendants actually lived on the premises.

was an actual observer of the terrible sins of Hophni and Phinehas at the tabernacle itself.

At the tabernacle, Samuel received the finest education possible. He also gained an appreciation for the importance of God's Word and the sinfulness of the priests and the people. God certainly provided the type of preparation that Samuel needed for his God-given work. There simply could have been no other place or way in which he could have been prepared as well.

One of the most important events in his young life was when God spoke to him (1 Samuel 3:2–14). One morning God simply called out Samuel's name. The boy could think only of Eli, his "father" and teacher, as the source of the call and ran quickly to him to ask what he wanted. This happened twice, and each time Eli told Samuel to return to his room—Eli had not called Samuel.

On the third time, however, Eli realized that the boy was not merely having a dream, but was actually being spoken to by God. Therefore, Eli told him that if he heard the call again to respond with the words, "Speak, Lord, for Your servant hears" (1 Samuel 3:9).

Once again, God called Samuel's name. This time Samuel did as Eli had instructed him. God then told Samuel that all that the "man of God" had told Eli earlier would truly come to pass. Because of the wickedness of Eli's sons, they would both be punished and the priesthood would be removed from Eli's family.

The next morning, Eli wanted to know exactly what God had said to Samuel. It must have been very hard for Samuel to tell Eli that God was going to bring punishment on his house and his sons because of their disobedience. However, Samuel told Eli what God had said. On hearing the news, Eli did not scold or punish Samuel. He simply said, "It is the Lord. Let Him do what seems good to Him" (1 Samuel 3:18).

Israel's Need for Leadership

After the death of Eli and his sons, Israel needed strong leadership. There was so much sin in the land that the morale of the people was at an all-time low. God specially prepared Samuel for this time. Samuel was to be God's leader during this time of national crisis.

Samuel quickly recognized the staggering challenge facing him as he became Israel's leader. First, he had to face the military challenges in the land. The Philistines had defeated Israel at Aphek. At the time, of course, Samuel had no way of knowing God's plan for disrupting the hopes of the Philistines through the work of Samson.

SAMUEL FACED TWO MAJOR CHALLENGES

- *The military challenge— the Philistines had to be defeated*

- *The sin challenge—the Israelites worshiped pagan gods.*

The second challenge facing Samuel was the terrible sins of the people. Samuel knew that the behavior of the people would not be changed quickly or easily. However, he also knew that God's blessing for victory could not be expected until that change took place.

One of Samuel's first tasks was to move the tabernacle from Shiloh to Nob. Once the tabernacle was moved to a safe place, Samuel took steps to address the people's sinfulness. Samuel did this by talking directly to the priests and challenging them to do the work to which God had called them. Samuel's message to the priests and Levites, that they were to in turn tell to the people, included the following:

- The tabernacle had been safely moved to Nob.

- Samuel had assumed the leadership as judge and that he intended to put an end to the sinfulness of the people.

- The priests and Levites were to get busy in their God-assigned task of instructing and guiding the people.

- The people were to stop worshiping the pagan gods and idols.

Of course, this was a difficult task for Samuel to accomplish by himself. Thus he established what has commonly been called the "school of the prophets." Although this term is not found in the Bible, a "group of prophets" is mentioned in 1 Samuel 10:5–10 and 19:20.

Samuel gathered his students from those who were concerned about the spiritual condition of Israel. The idea of a "school" came from his need to train them to help him carry out his work. Of course, Samuel was the teacher.

According to the Bible, it took Samuel nearly twenty years to accomplish this task. During these years, he traveled among the various cities of Israel to challenge the priests and Levites to resume their places of spiritual leadership. As he traveled from city to city, he trained his prophets to help him with the task. In addition to these responsibilities, he served as judge and leader in Israel.

Twenty years is a long time, especially when one has to overcome as many obstacles as Samuel did. There were probably many times that Samuel wanted to quit. However, Samuel did not give up. He continued on, in spite of his many discouragements, until he saw revival in the land of Israel.

Revival in Israel

As a result of Samuel's work, the nation of Israel experienced real revival as well as victory over the Philistines. The first report of the revival is recorded in 1 Samuel 7:4 where the Bible states, "So the children of Israel put away the Baals and the Ashtoreths, and served the Lord only." This action of the Israelites was not something that happened overnight. It was the result of Samuel's faithful ministry for twenty years.

As part of the revival, 1 Samuel 7:5–6 records that Samuel called all of the people together at a general assembly. The purpose was to demonstrate a collective show of repentance before God. To this call, "all Israel" is said to have responded, meaning that people from all parts of the land came to publicly confess their sins to God.

While this gathering of the people was taking place, the Philistines were planning an attack. As the Philistines drew near the assembled Israelites at Mizpah, the revival was at its height. When news reached the people that the Philistines were near, they became afraid. The people urged Samuel to call out to God for help.

Samuel immediately turned to God for deliverance. First Samuel 7:10 says that God "thundered with a loud thunder upon the

Philistines that day, and so confused them that they were overcome before Israel."

The time of year involved was probably during the dry season, when rainstorms and thunder were not expected. The Philistines were totally taken by surprise. The degree of the confusion must have been great because the Philistines turned and fled from the Israelites.

God does not always use armies to fight battles. In this case, He did the work by using thunder and rain, which probably was unusually severe. Israel reaped the benefit as the enemy turned in terror and ran. Israel won a decisive victory and the forty-year oppression of the Philistines was brought to an end.

LESSONS ON LEADERSHIP!

VIEWING OBSTACLES IN THE PROPER LIGHT

Samuel's First Lesson on Leadership!

If Samuel had been like most men, he would have seen the obstacles facing him and would have never accepted the position of leadership. If he had only focused on the obstacles, he would have been defeated before he even began his work.

But he looked beyond the obstacles and saw the greatness of God to conquer them. Of course, God wanted Samuel to lead. Since this was God's will for Samuel's life, God would take care of all the difficulties. Someone once said, "If God orders it, He will pay for it." This was certainly true for Samuel. All Samuel needed to do was trust God.

God is looking for leaders who will view every obstacle from His perspective. There is no obstacle too large for God.

1. A copy of the Ten Commandments, a copy of the entire Law of Moses, a gold pot filled with manna, and Aaron's rod that budded were contained in the ark of the covenant. Why do you believe God wanted each of these items included?

2. Samuel established the "school of the prophets." How does this demonstrate that Samuel was a good leader?

3. Research the meaning of the word revival. Identify examples of revivals in the Bible as well as in world history.

PREPARING FOR LEADERSHIP!

1. How was Samuel's preparation significant to the task God had given him?

2. As Samuel began to assume his place of leadership, what were the obstacles facing him?

3. Select one of the leaders (adult or student) at your school. What obstacles does this person face as he or she exercises leadership?

CHAPTER SEVENTEEN

Samuel

Anointing Saul as King

(1 Samuel 8–12)

After his victory over the Philistines at Mizpah, the Bible recorded that Samuel judged Israel for forty years. Very little is said about his work during this period, but we do know from 1 Samuel 7:15–17 that he traveled from city to city to carry on his work with the priests and the people. His regular contact with the people ensured that the revival that had begun at the beginning of his ministry would continue to bear fruit in the lives of the Israelites.

It was clearly during this time of lessened activity that Samuel made his two sons, Joel and Abijah, judges in Beersheba. Beersheba was far to the south of where Samuel lived. This area of Israel probably received little contact from Samuel, so Samuel sent his sons to provide leadership in his absence.

However, Samuel's sons did not follow in their father's godly footsteps. Instead, "they turned aside after dishonest gain, took bribes, and perverted justice" (1 Samuel 8:3). The people of the region were very angry with the actions of Samuel's sons. They no longer wanted the leadership of Joel and Abijah.

The People Request a King

The conduct of Samuel's sons once again caused the people to want a king. The idea behind this request had been building since the days of Gideon. Abimelech, as well as many of the minor judges, had lived a kingly lifestyle. Now, finally an actual request for a king for all the land of Israel was brought to Samuel.

It was God's desire that the people accept Him as their king. This was known as a theocracy. God knew that a theocracy would have worked if the people had met the one requirement of obedience. Because they would not obey, God permitted them to have a king.

The people would now have a second-best form of government—a king—because they had rejected the best.

The people's request for a king was both proper and improper. It was improper in the sense that the people rejected God as their king. God had entrusted them with the theocratic form of government

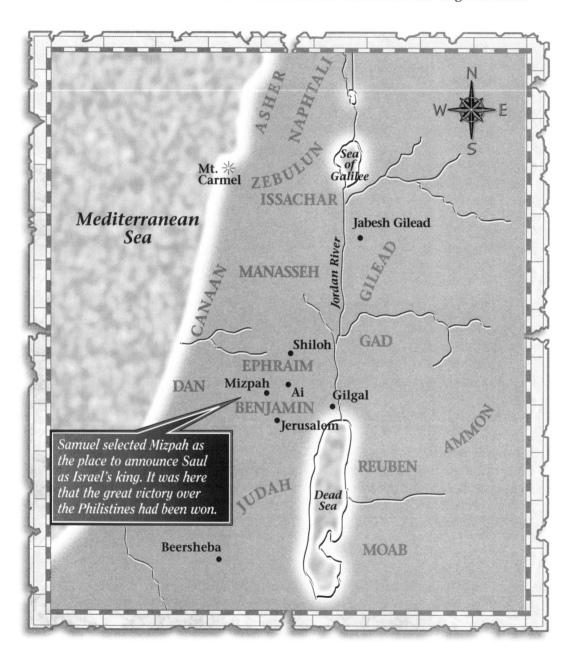

Samuel selected Mizpah as the place to announce Saul as Israel's king. It was here that the great victory over the Philistines had been won.

and the people said, by their actions, that they did not want it. In no place in all the world had a people been given the blessing of this form of rule before, and they rejected it. The Israelites wanted a monarchy instead.

The request was proper in that, because of the sinful conditions of the time, the people were now better off with an earthly ruler. As the Bible clearly explained, every man was doing "what was right in his own eyes" (Judges 17:6). This sinfulness of the people created chaos in the land. Because of these circumstances, God instructed Samuel to give them the king that they had requested.

When the request first came, Samuel was terribly hurt. It seemed to him that the people were rejecting *him* after he had worked for so many years on their behalf. It appeared that they did not appreciate the great effort he put forth to save the country.

God reassured Samuel that he was not really the one being rejected, but that it was *God Himself*. He further told Samuel that, because of the sinful conditions among the people, it actually would be better if the people now had a king (1 Samuel 8:8–9).

God told Samuel to make sure that the people understood that heavy demands and taxes would be imposed on them by their chosen king. The people of Israel had not been under such restrictions before, but that was about to change. God wanted the people to know how much better His plan for them had been. They would now be getting only a second-best form of rule. Samuel carried out God's instructions, but the people said they still wanted a king. Samuel then proceeded to secure one for them, under God's continued guidance.

BIBLE BACKGROUND

Theocracy

A theocracy refers to direct government of the nation of Israel by God Himself or His earthly representatives. Although theocracy is not a Biblical word, the concept of God's rule on earth is thoroughly Biblical. In a theocracy, human rulers interpret and carry out the divine ruler's will. In Israel's early days, God ruled through men such as Moses, Aaron, and Joshua. Later, God ruled the nation by using the various judges. Now the nation of Israel would be ruled by an earthly king.

Establishment of Saul as King

The person God selected as Israel's first king was Saul, son of Kish, a Benjamite. Saul was a fine physical man, taller than the average person (1 Samuel 9:2), and this was helpful in making him acceptable to the people.

Not everyone in Israel wanted a king. Samuel knew there would be a problem getting a majority of the people to agree on the identity of the person chosen to be king. A king can rule only when he is recognized in that capacity by the people. Therefore, Saul's kingly appearance helped solve this problem.

God first revealed to Samuel that He had selected Saul as king. Saul then learned from Samuel that he had been divinely chosen to serve as Israel's first king. Certainly, this must have been a great surprise to Saul.

BIBLE BACKGROUND

The United and Divided Kingdom

The twelve tribes of Israel were united under kings Saul, David, and Solomon. After the death of Solomon in 922, the kingdom divided into a southern kingdom called the kingdom of Judah and a northern kingdom called the kingdom of Israel. The tribes of Judah and Benjamin comprised the southern kingdom. The other ten tribes made up the northern kingdom. The books of 1, 2 Kings and 1, 2 Chronicles describe the nation's history during this time of the divided kingdom.

It was one thing to inform Saul that he had been selected as king. It was quite another thing to inform the leaders of Israel of God's selection. Samuel selected Mizpah as the place to announce Saul as Israel's king. It was here that the great victory over the Philistines had been won. When Saul was announced as God's choice, he was accepted with great shouts of approval.

Although Saul had been accepted by the leaders, he still needed the recognition of the people in general. Saul needed an opportunity to demonstrate his leadership. His opportunity came when he led the Israelites to victory over the Ammonites. The Ammonites, defeated by Jephthah forty years earlier, had recently attacked the city of Jabesh Gilead. Saul took advantage of this occasion to gain the recognition he needed. He was able to gather a large army and then lead the troops in a decisive victory, thus saving Jabesh Gilead and making himself famous all across the land. The people were now willing to accept him, and he was crowned king of Israel at Gilgal.

Samuel's Final Words to the People

After Saul was crowned king, Samuel delivered his final message to the people (1 Samuel 12:1–25). It must have been an emotional moment for the aged prophet and retiring judge. He had worked diligently for the country all of his life. Now he was stepping down in favor of a king for which the people had asked.

Samuel knew that the anointing of a king would not solve Israel's problems. The nation's sinful behavior had to change. If not, the monarchy was doomed to failure.

Samuel reminded the people of his own righteous conduct among them. He then reviewed their past failures and strongly urged them to ask God for forgiveness and change their behavior. He told them that if they would obey God, they would enjoy His blessings. Then, as a way of stressing this truth, he called on God to send a thunderstorm (1 Samuel 12:17). God answered the call, and the people cried out in fear as the miraculous thunder rolled and the rain fell. Samuel once again challenged the people to forsake their sins and obey God. He then promised that he would continue to pray for the people.

With the anointing of Saul as king, the period of the judges ended. Now Israel had a king, like other nations. Saul, David, and then Solomon would lead Israel during the time known as "the united monarchy." This was a time when all of the tribes of Israel were ruled by the same king.

LESSONS ON LEADERSHIP!

MAINTAINING ONE'S HONOR

Samuel's Second Lesson on Leadership!

Although Samuel was hurt by the people's request for a king, he did not try to get even with them for making this choice. God had revealed to him that it was time for the people to have their earthly king. As God's servant, Samuel humbly accepted their decision and God's plan. The Bible describes Samuel as "a man of God, and . . . an honorable man" (1 Samuel 9:6).

It is often easy to rebel or seek revenge when things don't go your way. But as Samuel clearly realized, God is in control of all that happens. Godly leadership demands that we maintain our honor, no matter what happens. Our response to every situation we face is to do what's right! If we will humbly seek God's guidance, He will direct our decisions.

INCREASE YOUR UNDERSTANDING

1. Saul reigned as king over all of Israel. Yet, a few years later, Israel became a divided kingdom with kings in the north and in the south. Why did this happen?

2. How would the requirements on the typical Israelite change under the rule of a king?

3. Judges 17:6 says that every man was doing "what was right in his own eyes." Give three specific examples of how this verse could describe people today.

PREPARING FOR LEADERSHIP!

Dr. Mark Lee, educator and author, has said, "Persons who lead earn the right to lead as they respond to the opportunities God places before them." Explain how Samuel's life illustrates this important principle. Describe how this principle can be applied in your own life.

CHAPTER EIGHTEEN

What Have We Learned?

God is in control of history. He who created the world will not let the world move out from under His supreme guidance at any time. This does not mean that all that happens is pleasing to God. Much of what happens is permitted by God, but He is still in control. One of the fascinating reasons for studying history is to observe how God's hand is continually at work.

Not only is God in control of today's events, He has also been in control of the events in the past. This is particularly true in the history of His chosen people, the Israelites. Nothing has happened in the history of Israel that was not under God's special direction. Of course, this includes the period of the judges.

The book of Judges, and the period it spans, is unlike any other time in Israel's history. It explains what happened in the life of the Israelites from the time they entered the Promised Land until they anointed Saul as their first king. Not only is the history interesting, but there are many valuable lessons to learn from each of the individuals we encounter. Let's take a few moments to review what we have learned.

A Time of Transition

The first six books of the Bible explain the beginning of the nation of Israel, how the nation became so large, and then the journey to the Promised Land.

The book of Judges is the seventh book of the Old Testament. It describes a transitional period in the life of Israel. Its title comes from the twelve men and one woman who served as judges during the time from Joshua's death to the installment of Israel's first king, Saul. None of the judges were national leaders as Moses and Joshua had been. They were common individuals who had been specifically chosen by God to provide deliverance from Israel's enemies and leadership to the people. The time between Israel's arrival in the Promised Land and the anointing of King Saul is called the "period of the judges."

The second important period in Israel's history (immediately following the period of the judges) is called the time of the monarchy or the "kingdom period." It is the time when the nation was directly under the rule of kings—some good and some evil. The book of Judges was written during the time of the monarchy. It is possible that it was written by Samuel, but the actual author is unknown.

The Beginning of the Nation of Israel
Genesis, Exodus, Leviticus, Numbers, Deuteronomy, Joshua

Transition to a King
Judges

The Nation of Israel Ruled by Kings
1, 2 Samuel; 1, 2 Kings; 1, 2 Chronicles

Judges Were Needed Because of Israel's Sins

The children of Israel entered the Promised Land with high hopes. God had delivered them out of bondage in Egypt, led them through the wilderness for forty years, and brought them into a land that they could call their own. Time after time, over those many years, God had demonstrated His power to protect and provide for them.

In return for His protection and provision, God wanted Israel's devotion and obedience. But this did not happen. The book of Judges is the story of Israel's cycle of sin and deliverance.

This cycle of sin and deliverance began with the nation serving God. Then they took steps downward. The Israelites did evil in the sight of the Lord and served the Baals (Judges 2:11). They forsook the Lord, and they served the Baals and the Ashtoreths. The anger of the Lord was hot against Israel, and He delivered the nation into the hands of its enemies. Israel entered a time of bondage to the oppressing nation. Soon Israel cried out to God for help. The Israelites turned to God and repented. God heard their prayers and raised up judges through whom the nation was delivered. Then Israel once again served God.

For a while, the nation was at peace. Soon the same old story repeated itself. The children of Israel did evil, forsook God, followed their own pleasures, were sold into slavery, entered a period of bondage, cried out to God for help, turned to Him, judges were raised up, and then Israel was delivered. The nation began serving God again, and Israel was once again at the top of the cycle. The old saying "history repeats itself" was certainly true of Israel during the time of the judges.

Israel's Cycle of Sin and Deliverance

- The Nation Served God
- The Nation Did Evil
- The Nation Forsook God
- The Nation Followed Its Own Way (Pleasure)
- The Nation Was Sold into Slavery (Depression and War)
- The Nation in Slavery
- The Nation in Servitude
- The Nation Cried Out to God
- The Nation Turned to God
- The Nation Repented
- God Raised Up Judges
- The Nation Was Delivered

Who Were These Judges?

As we have learned, the judges described in the book of Judges were not like those we see in today's courtrooms. In the book of Judges, a "judge" was an individual who "served as a leader." Although this leadership might involve deciding disputes between individuals, it might also involve serving in local government or as a military leader.

Each of the judges was an ordinary person whom God used in a special way to lead His people. They served as leaders of the people of Israel from the time they entered the Promised Land until Saul was anointed as king—a period of almost four hundred years!

THE JUDGES, AND THE NATIONS THAT OPPRESSED ISRAEL DURING THEIR TIME OF LEADERSHIP

Name	Oppression	Reference
Othniel	Mesopotamians	Judges 3:7–11
Ehud	Moabites	Judges 3:12–30
Shamgar		Judges 3:31
Deborah with Barak	Canaanites	Judges 4–5
Gideon	Midianites	Judges 6–8
Tola		Judges 10:1–2
Jair		Judges 10:3–5
Jephthah	Ammonites	Judges 10:6–12:7
Ibzan		Judges 12:8–10
Elon		Judges 12:11–12
Abdon		Judges 12:13–15
Samson	Philistines	Judges 13–16

As we saw in chapters 16 and 17, Bible scholars believe that Samuel was the last to serve in the capacity of a judge. He served as a transitional leader between the close of the period of the judges and the beginning of the monarchy under King Saul.

At the time Samuel became the leader in Israel, the nation was in terrible condition. The priesthood had become corrupt and the worship at the tabernacle no longer honored God. The sinfulness of the people of Israel was great. The country became completely dependent upon the Philistines and freely worshiped their pagan gods.

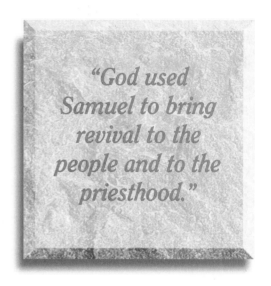

"God used Samuel to bring revival to the people and to the priesthood."

However, God had not abandoned Israel. He raised up Samuel as the one who would lead the people out of their bondage of sin and dependence upon the Philistines. God used Samuel to bring revival to the people and to the priesthood. Samuel anointed Saul as king, uniting the nation of Israel for the first time in over four hundred years.

The Story Continues . . .

Although the story described in the book of Judges ended three thousand years ago, the cycle of sin and deliverance continues. History has shown that when a nation ignores God and turns away from Biblical morality, it deteriorates to the point of destruction. In the course of history, there have been many revivals and times of spiritual awakenings that have caused nations to repent of their sins and turn back to God.

Revival: "a period of renewed religious interest."

Just as God raised up deliverers in the past, He is raising up deliverers today. Are you willing to take your place as one of God's leaders for the next generation?

FAMOUS REVIVALS AROUND THE WORLD

Name	Location	Dates	Leaders	Description
Mediaeval Monastic Revivals	Italy and Western Europe	950–1350	Benedict of Aniane Berno of Cluny Robert of Citeaux Bernard of Clairvaux Bruno of Chartreuse Robert of Arbrissel Francis of Assisi Dominic of Castile	Fresh outbreaks of revival offset the indifference and corruption of the Catholic Church. Most movements either separated from the pagan society or penetrated society with the Gospel.
The Reformation	Western Europe	1517–1575	Martin Luther John Calvin Huldreich Zwingli John Knox Philip Melanchthon Thomas Cranmer	Efforts to reform growing corruption within the Roman Catholic Church resulted in revival, a major break with the church, and a return to the doctrines of "Scripture alone," "grace alone," and "faith alone."
Puritan Awakening	England and America	1610–1640	Thomas Cartwright Robert Browne John Cotton John Winthrop	The "New Light" Puritans revolted against the "Old Light" Church of England. The revival sought the spiritual purification of the Anglican Church from the corruption left over from its Catholic roots.
German Puritan Revival	Germany	1666–1750	John Arndt Philip Jacob Spener August Francke Nicolaus Ludwig of Zinsendorf	Following the Thirty Year's War, this religious awakening drew from the mysticism of pietism. Cultivating the Christian life through prayer and Bible study, the revival encouraged moral and spiritual reformation.

FAMOUS REVIVALS AROUND THE WORLD (Continued)

Name	Location	Dates	Leaders	Description
First Great Awakening	America	1730–1760	Jonathan Edwards George Whitefield Gilbert Tennent	The demographic, economic, and intellectual changes of colonial America challenged the moral and spiritual well-being of the colonists. The mercy of a stern and angry God brought sinners to salvation.
Wesleyan Revival	England	1738–1815	John Wesley Charles Wesley George Whitefield	Fired by the zeal of their conversions and the joy of their conscious salvation, the Wesleyan revivalists preached the Gospel of faith in Christ alone.
Second Great Awakening	America	1800–1830	Timothy Dwight Lyman Beecher Nathaniel W. Taylor Charles Finney	In the years following the Revolution, the American people began to wonder if they would realize their full potential. A multitude of doubts made them ripe for revival.
African Revival	Central Africa	1800–1900	Robert Moffat David Livingstone George Grenfell Alexander Mackay Mary Slessor	Through great sacrifice, missionaries carried the Gospel to the African continent. Using trade and technology to overcome fearful resistance, this movement brought Africa to Christ.
Layman's Prayer Meeting Revival	America, Canada, Western Europe, and South Africa	1857–1858	Jeremiah C. Lanphier George B. Cheever J. W. Alexander William Adams Edward N. Kirk	With important changes occurring in technology and mass communications, a number of businessmen began prayer meetings seeking God's direction. Revival followed.

Name	Location	Dates	Leaders	Description
Chinese Revival	China	1865–1905	Robert Morrison J. Hudson Taylor	Revival came to China years after the first seed had been planted. The evangelical China Inland Mission benefitted from sound organization and close identification with the Chinese people.
Third Great Awakening	America	1890–1920	Dwight L. Moody Billy Sunday	Mass revivals saw thousands of converts as America struggled through the post-Civil War adjustments and the challenge of liberal theology.
Korean Pentecost	Korea	1906–1910	John L. Nevius R. A. Hardie Graham Lee W. L. Swallen W. B. Hunt S. C. Kil	Although Christianity had been introduced to Korea centuries before, it had nearly been exterminated. This revival saw the church in Korea grow to become a Christian nation.
Indonesian Revivals	Indonesia	1916–1922 and 1965–1970	Pieter Middelkoop J. A. Ratuwalu Benjamin Manuain Detmar Scheunemann	These 20th-century revivals were accompanied by a fear of God's judgment, a break with demonic forces, visions, prophecies, public confession of sin, prayer, miracle phenomena, and a team approach to evangelism.
Fourth Great Awakening	America	1960–1990	Billy Graham Bill Bright Louis Palau	The crisis of living in the modern world after World War II, including the loss of values and the growth of materialism, left many seeking for significance. A Gospel revival answered the failure of liberal theology to give meaning and hope to life.

In 2 Chronicles 7:14, God outlines the path a nation must take in order to be blessed by God. As you consider God's prescription for a nation's success described in the following verse, ask yourself how this verse applies to your walk with the Lord and future role as a Christian leader.

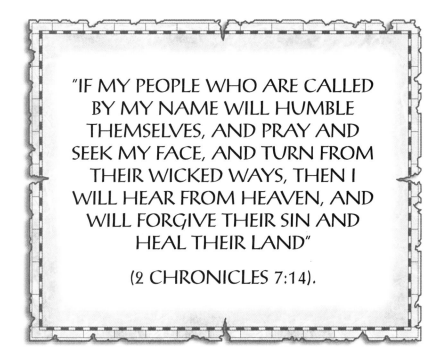

"IF MY PEOPLE WHO ARE CALLED BY MY NAME WILL HUMBLE THEMSELVES, AND PRAY AND SEEK MY FACE, AND TURN FROM THEIR WICKED WAYS, THEN I WILL HEAR FROM HEAVEN, AND WILL FORGIVE THEIR SIN AND HEAL THEIR LAND"

(2 CHRONICLES 7:14).

NOTES

DARING DELIVERERS

NOTES

NOTES

DARING DELIVERERS

NOTES

NOTES

DARING DELIVERERS